THE BOY WHO CATCHES WASPS

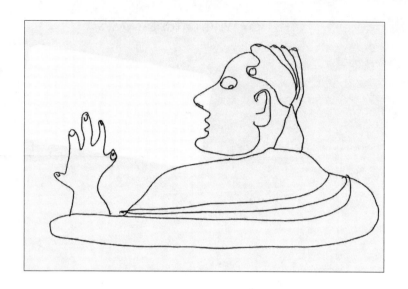

THE BOY WHO CATCHES WASPS

DUO DUO

TRANSLATED FROM THE CHINESE
BY GREGORY B. LEE

ZEPHYR PRESS
BROOKLINE, MA

Publication was assisted by a grant from the Tiny Tiger Foundation, the Massachusetts Cultural Council, and the National Endowment for the Arts.

NATIONAL ENDOWMENT FOR THE ARTS

MASSACHUSETTS CULTURAL COUNCIL

Cover illustration and drawings throughout the text by Duo Duo
Cover and book design by *typeslowly*
Chinese typesetting by Ling-Chun Lee and Jody Beenk
Printed in Canada

Library of Congress Control Number: 2002104100

98765432 FIRST PRINTING IN 2002
       ZEPHYR PRESS
50 KENWOOD STREET   BROOKLINE, MA 02446
       www.zephyrpress.org

REVERIE, EXILE, AND THE CRITIQUE OF MODERN LIFE

Duo Duo left China for a reading tour of England the morning of June 4th 1989, after the night of the Tiananmen massacre he had witnessed. The poetry readings had been planned long before, but the poet had never imagined how the turn of events of that Chinese year of the Snake would change the course of his life and poetry.

I first met Duo Duo in the final hours of 1985. I had read his poetry in samizdat publications, and in his work I found a complexity of imagery and syntax absent in the work of most post-Mao generation poets. Through an intermediary I invited Duo Duo to celebrate the New Year at my apartment in Beijing. We talked poetry well into the dawn of New Year's Day, 1986. I recall we discussed his contemporaries Bei Dao, Gu Cheng, Mang Ke, Jiang He. I remember arguing about the importance of the contribution made to modern Chinese poetry by its pioneering inventors of the 1920s and 1930s; I had just finished a book on the early twentieth-century francophile poet Dai Wangshu. But mostly we talked about European and American poets. By the time of our encounter, Duo Duo had been writing for around fifteen years, having committed his first tentative, terse verses to paper in the early 1970s when the Cultural Revolution was in full swing. Of course, he was obliged to write clandestinely, never imagining he would one day have readers. He continued to write throughout the 1980s, publishing in samizdat publications, and then more openly as the cultural authorities relaxed their grip. The reading tour in 1989 was Duo Duo's first trip outside of China.

A year or so after Duo Duo's arrival in Europe, around the time he turned forty, he wrote a story entitled "Going Home," which concerns a young Chinese man who takes a bus to a small English seaside town where he proceeds to spend the rest of his life. The story constructs a space within which is represented the confused and scattered detritus of political and cultural dreams and nightmares of modernity, and the beginnings of an attempt to reimagine by what Bachelard has called "reveries of will" (*les rêveries de la volonté*) the narratives which constituted twentieth-century history in China and elsewhere.[1]

Twentieth-century Chinese cultural and intellectual history can be read as a linear history which parallels the history of China's efforts to compensate for the effects of the technological and economic uneven development so brutally foregrounded by Western and Japanese, but in particular British imperialist aggression in "opening up" China.

Central to the inventing of China's modernity has been the rebuilding of the Chinese language. By a willful action of textual production, China's writers sought to reinvent China as a modern nation-state. They employed fiction writing as a didactic and political weapon. But it was poetry that had dominated the literary scene in China for over two thousand years, and thus, a new poetry was essential to the prestige of the new literature. New language, new forms, new modes were prescribed to overcome the formalistic legacy of modes of lyric writing become anachronistic at the end of the nineteenth century. From the second decade of the twentieth century onwards, modern poets nurtured and shaped a new poetry. By the mid 1940s a new poetic language with which to engage modernity had become fully and powerfully available. But the advent of People's China in 1949, and with it the tutelage of the bureaucratic state and the rhythmic certainty of socio-cultural instabilities diverted and warped the new language. After the passing of Mao, the party-state's hegemony over language and literature became increasingly contested, and from the mid 1970s onwards, the process of language creation, reinvention, and renovation began again. It is to this most recent period of poetic and linguistic invention that the poet Duo Duo has made a major contribution over the past thirty years. For half of that time Duo Duo's writing has taken place in exile.

The character Lee in Duo Duo's story "Going Home" is a Chinese who finds himself in exile. Lee had gone to live in a village on the northeast coast of England. At the beginning of this story we find him waiting for the arrival of another Chinese. He seems to have waited forty years:

Many years have passed, and whether I have spoken or not spoken with the townsfolk has become equally unimportant; they have aged with me amidst our unchanging relations, and the children of the youngsters who used to call me Lee still call me Lee today. Sometimes, when they come to visit their parents buried beneath the earth, I stand with them for a while....

Like this country cemetery and this church, my arrival and stay have long lost their rationale; or, that rationale has long lost its flavor. I tend to the flowers and foliage throughout the year, and as long as it is not raining, I go to the fields to watch the sky. If it is raining, I stay in; but if there is a storm, then I must go out. In the storm, I sit on the bench of the church across from the town square and holding a red umbrella. At those times, behind the shop windows, the people speak: look, that Chinese is waiting again.

What they say is perfectly correct; I am waiting. I am waiting for the arrival of another Chinese. I think he must be a young man, perhaps with a backpack, perhaps without. Emerging from the long-distance bus depot, he will pass a second-hand bookstore and walk straight into the square; he will see me in the rain and approach me, and listen to the tale I tell him. If he is willing to listen, then I shall be able to depart from this world; or, as the Chinese say, I shall be able to go home....

But while "waiting for the arrival of another Chinese," what sense is to be made of the world of exile in which China and Chineseness is constituted by fragments of memories, of restaurant signboards, of scraps of Chinese writing, and garish-colored picture calendars? In Duo Duo's story, China is felt in its absence and by traces, appearances, and presences that fail to translate into a cogent sense of Chineseness.

The muteness represented here, the lack of power to enunciate, could be read as a reference to the modern Chinese subject's incapacity to interrogate itself, of China's inability to imagine itself otherwise than as an entity mimicking the West. Not just the non-communication of China after 1989, of China after Mao, after 1949, but even further back, China after colonialism, China after the white man. The Chinese is powerless to speak, only able to be spoken in the vocabulary of globalized daily life. The Chinese restaurant owner cannot speak, will not speak. This "Chinese" space, this space that calls itself Chinese and yet is located in an English village, a global village. This Chinese space is empty of meaning, of the capacity to communicate, except for a visual representation, a spatial and temporal window, the Western painting of a Chinese landscape. A representation of a physicality and territoriality of China, somewhere, some time. Not a reality, an unreality, a dreamed painting.

"I never dream in England," declares the narrator Lee. But to produce no dreams is to produce no poetry, and unlike his narrator, after his arrival in Europe, Duo Duo did dream and did write poems. The early exile poems were very much poems haunted by the national and personal tragedies the poet had left behind, but also by the new-found sadness of exile. They are poems of mourning and loss, poems in which China figures once more as an absence, as in the poem "The Rivers of Amsterdam" written in 1989:

> November as the city enters night
> there are only the rivers of Amsterdam
>
> suddenly
>
> the mandarins on the tree at home
> quiver in the autumn breeze
>
> ....
>
> after the passing of the autumn rain
> that roof crawling with snails
> — my motherland
>
> on Amsterdam's rivers, slowly sailing by...

When still in China, Duo Duo was attracted by the resistance to the routine of modern programmed existence that he found in the reveries of the West's modernist poets, in Baudelaire and in Lorca, in Dylan Thomas, in David Gascoyne, but more sonorously in the poetry of Marina Tsvetaeva, and Sylvia Plath. But, once in the West, Duo Duo's imagined poetic universe was made to confront the materiality, the lived experience of Western realities and Western ideologies.

In 1989, the poetic dream of living otherwise was not transferred from China to England, it was deferred. The experience of the West's modernity replaced innocent anticipation, 1989's dreams of emancipation, with the anxiety of having to reimagine, to dream again. Anxiety, and mourning and the insistent importance assigned to death and the dead:

> With no dead, the river can have no end…

In Duo Duo's poetry, tropes of death, of the space of the dead occur repeatedly. "If dream is a reminiscence, it is the reminiscence of a state preceding life, of a state of *dead* life, a kind of mourning before happiness," wrote Bachelard.[2] Dream translates the desire to live rather than merely to survive, before the finality of Death itself. Thus Dylan Thomas's refusal "to go gentle into that good night", thus the poet's railing resistance to Death's dominion.[3]

If dream *is* a reminiscence, "a kind of mourning before happiness," then the imperative to mourn before happiness is not confined to dreams of China, and while it might seem reasonable to perceive in Duo Duo's concern with death as merely a contemplation of China's modern tragedies such a reading would be erroneous. Duo Duo's poetic vision embraces a historical and political vision that is much more diverse, more global than that circumscribed by the contextual confines of the last third of China's twentieth century. The context of China, Duo Duo's lived experience, is necessarily present in the poet's imaginary, but it is diffused in a world-view that embraces all of modern humanity's dilemmas, our increasing separation from Nature, and our alienation from one another. The exile, like the hybrid and other marginal and "in-between" subjects, writes of China with the benefit of critical distance, but also writes with an exceptional perspective of wherever he finds himself. Witness the observations of the exiled "I" in these verses:

Often they occupy a metal chair in the park, these women
Just as they often own many clothes
In the houses they own lives have also been lived
This town is often dreamt of by them
This world is also

....

They want to listen closely now, whether to people
To animals, or to rivers, often
They feel themselves to be the same port
Waiting for boats to leave or arrive
They do not necessarily want to go to Africa
But rather to sit on that regular metal chair
The exile opposite them can only cover up with apple tree leaves
And sleep, sleep and dream
It's as if their wombs were tomorrow's church.

1992

The reader will find in these pages, then, a poetry in which the societal is entwined with the individual, and the Chinese enmeshed in the global. It is above all a poetry which filters lived experience through the prism of the subconscious, which restores to its rightful place the importance of dream, of reverie; a poetry in which "oneiric forces ceaselessly flow into conscious life."[4]

Gregory B. Lee

[1] Gaston Bachelard, *La terre et les rêveries de la volonté* (Paris: José Corti, 1948, 1965).
[2] Gaston Bachelard, *L'Air et les Songes* as translated in Bachelard, *On Poetic Imagination and Reverie*, translated by Colette Gaudin, (Dallas, TX: Spring Publications, 1987, 1994) 14.
[3] Dylan Thomas, "Death Shall Have No Dominion" in Collected Poems 1934-1952 (London: Dent, 1952, 1972) 62.
[4] Bachelard, *Poetic Imagination and Reverie* 13.

I append this note to my translations of Duo Duo's in the hope that it may provide the non-Chinese speaking reader with an idea of what is involved in the translation of a contemporary Chinese poem, and of the inevitable choices that have to be made given the complexity and ambiguity of the poetry of Duo Duo.

The reason for such complexity is in part a result of the poet's espousal of the aesthetics of modernism, which in the twentieth century knew no frontiers, but it is also largely a function of the political and linguistic particularities of the historical moment in which the "unofficial contemporary poetry" of Communist-era China was written. With the advent of the People's Republic of China came official control of literary production and a standardization of the language. The highpoint of this logic of centralized and bureaucrat control came with the Cultural Revolution (1966-76) when literature was being beaten into a tool for propaganda, and language was industrialized into a Maoist elaboration of Orwellian 'Newspeak,' a language which not only pervaded cultural life, but which also dominated all aspects of daily life, thought and action. Rather than encouraging the people to learn to make their own literature, the supposedly egalitarian Cultural Revolution privileged the training of model worker-writers who churned out verses to the glory of Mao, the Party, the Motherland, and the industrial domination of Nature. The role of poetry was not to imagine mythically, but to reproduce a unique and official myth. This official versifying was totally at the service of ideology, it was poetry become "civil litany" as Benjamin Péret once said of French Communist wartime poetry.

It was in this context of servitude to the revolutionary motherland that the "unofficial poetry," given the sobriquet "misty" or obscure" poetry by the authorities, was born. For the young urban poets, often former Red Guards born to good families, and now disillusioned with Maoist ideology, poetry constituted the means of contesting the official, and officially inspired narratives of modern history. This new poetry represented the story of a personally lived reality interpreted from individual perspectives. It was above all a reinvention of the language that a number of young writers chose to negotiate and re-tell the past, contest the present and imagine the future. Expressing the necessity to denaturalize and remodel literary language in post-Mao China, Duo Duo wrote:

With refashioned tools refashion language

But how was language to be refashioned? The monosyllabic nature of the Chinese language dictates that new words can only be created by juxtaposing existing characters, each character having a monosyllabic phonetic value and each in itself a word, to create new polysyllabic words. It is rare in Chinese for new characters to be invented (except, say, for the naming of new chemical elements), and their invention is hardly necessary given the 50,000 or more existing characters. Thus, it is at the level of syntactical manipulation and metaphoric creation that the Chinese poet can be inventive. Duo Duo does this by pushing the meaning of words and the limits of ambiguity further and further, and by employing words in combinations unthinkable in the language of officialdom and daily routine.

A number of aspects of the Chinese language assist the poet in his quest to reinvent and denaturalize his own poetic language. By exploiting these possibilities, he can invest his poem with ambiguity, play on words, and turn phrases thus opening up new planes of sense, which push the reader to think differently about his own language. This linguistic latitude and opacity is reinforced by the fact that Chinese, like Spanish, does not insist on the consistent use of the personal pronoun, and by the fact that, unlike Spanish, there is no indication at all of the subject of the verb contained within the verb itself. The Chinese verb does not conjugate and indeed gives no indication of tense, while the Chinese noun is not declined and has no gender. All these aspects of the Chinese language augment the possibilities for ambiguity; a lack of "precision" which may perturb the modern scientist but not the modernist poet.

Here is an example of one of Duo Duo's poems, "In the Grave-yard," in a first rough English version showing the array of literal translations available. I provide the *pinyin* phonetic transliteration first, and the reader may also refer to the Chinese character version on page 140.

Zai mudi, er meiyou huiyi
you hanxi, danshi bei tuichi
mengzhe lian, wei xia qu

chang :

mei ren yao women, women zai yiqi
shi women beihou de yun, yao women kao zai yiqi
women beihou de shu, bici kao de geng jin

chang

yinwei shouru
xue cong tianshang lai, yinwei zhufu
feng zai cidi, cidi bian shi yiwang
yue shi yuan li maidi, bian yue shi gudu

shouting

ranhou shouge, hanleng, cai bozhong
renshou, suoyi jingjiu
xiangxin, yushi duchu :

you

you yige feixiang de jia —— zai zhao women

in the cemetery, but/and there is/are no memory/memories
there is/are (a) sigh(s), but postponed
cover(ing) face(s)/face(s) covered, kneel(ing) down

sing/singing :

nobody wants us, we are together
it's the cloud(s) behind us, that want(s) us to huddle together
the trees behind us, huddle even closer
sing(ing)

Because humiliated
Snow comes from the sky, because blessing/blessed
The wind (is) in this place, this place is therefore forget(ting)
The further the wheat field, the lonelier

Listen(s)/listening

And then harvest, ice cold, only then sow(s)
endure(s)/enduring/suffer(s)/suffering, thus last(s)/lasting
believe(s)/believing, then recite(s)/reciting

(there) is/are/has/have

(there) is/are/has/have a home —— busy looking for us

To make sense of such a poem the reader needs to read and re-
read several times, since as the poem progresses the meaning of the
earlier stanzas may be altered or enriched. In the very first stanza, where
the reader might expect some direction, there is instead disorienta-
tion. There are several ambiguities. There is a total absence of personal
pronouns, and no indication of number. It is thus unclear whether
there is one "sigh" or several which cover(s) the face, which kneel(s)
down. But whose face, and who or what kneels down? Perhaps it is the

voice of the poem who acts. And then who sings? The second stanza seems to give some clues. There is a pronoun: "we" (*women*) employed five times in the Chinese. But to whom or what does this "we" refer? Surely it refers to the plural voice of the poem? But what if it refers to the "sighs" of the first stanza? There is another almost imperceptible pointer. The word "sing(ing)" between the first and second full stanzas is followed by a colon. The use of punctuation, foregrounded by its sparseness in Duo Duo's poetry, does not always provide a clarification of the sense of a given line of poetry. But the commas, semi-colons and periods sometimes found in the middle of a line do usually limit the amplitude of its ambiguity. Here the colon seems to suggest that it is the subject of the first stanza that sings, and that the second stanza can be taken as direct speech. There is, however, still the question of whether the subject of the first stanza is a nebulous "we": people, or the dead? Or is it indeed the "sighs" which sing? The word *chang*, "sing," also appears again between the second and third stanzas, but this second time is not followed by a colon, and no pronoun occurs in the third stanza. Does the word *chang* simply close the direct speech of the preceding stanza, and should it therefore be translated by the gerund "singing"?

In the third stanza, who or what is "humiliated"? Is the subject still the voice of the poem, or an undeclared subject? Or is it the "snow" that is humiliated? The syntax would allow such an interpretation. Again does the snow come from the sky because it is blessed, or is it the wind that is blessed? Do the "sighs" still constitute the subject? And who or what is "lonely"?

Between the third and fourth stanzas is the word *shouting*, "listen (in)" or more literally "listen-receive"; the character *shou* ("receive") occurs again in the first verse of the fourth stanza: *Ranhou shouge...* ("And then afterward harvest...") where *shouge* more literally means "receive-cut." The translator is faced with the question of how to render this repetition of a character-syllable embedded in two different words.

Again in this fourth full stanza, it is still impossible to define the subject. Do "we suffer" or do "they suffer," do "we believe" or do "they"? And then the stanza ends with a colon, which seems to indicate that again there follows direct speech the subject of which, "we," is revealed only in the last line of the poem.

The interest of this poem resides in the ambiguity of the subject. In reading this poem in Chinese the reader can preserve its multiple significations, return to what is previously read, and substitute meanings. Of course, an easily readable translation is possible, but it is precisely such a closed reading that the translator must resist. Therein lies the thorniness of the task: the translator is obliged to produce a seamless version while attempting to leave to the non-Chinese reader the autonomy to supply a plurality of meaning.

Here is my polished version of the poem discussed above:

IN THE GRAVEYARD

In the graveyard, and there are no recollections
There are sighs, but they are deferred
Faces covered, kneeling down

Singing:

No one wants us, we are together
It's the clouds behind us, want us to huddle together
The trees behind us, huddle even closer

Singing

Since humiliated
Snow comes from the sky, since fortunate
The wind is here, so here is forgetting
The further from the wheat field, the lonelier

Listening in

Then gathering in, icy cold, then sowing
Enduring, therefore durable
Believing, thereupon read out:

There is

There is a home with wings —— seeking us out.

1992

I leave the last and wisest word to my erstwhile teacher and master translator of the classical Chinese language, the late Angus Graham:

"The translator of a complex text is a juggler with a dozen balls to keep in the air in simultaneous flight, and some of them are always bouncing on the floor." [§]

[§] *Chuang-Tzu: The Inner Chapters* (London and Boston: Unwin Hyman, 1989), p.33.

THE BOY WHO CATCHES WASPS

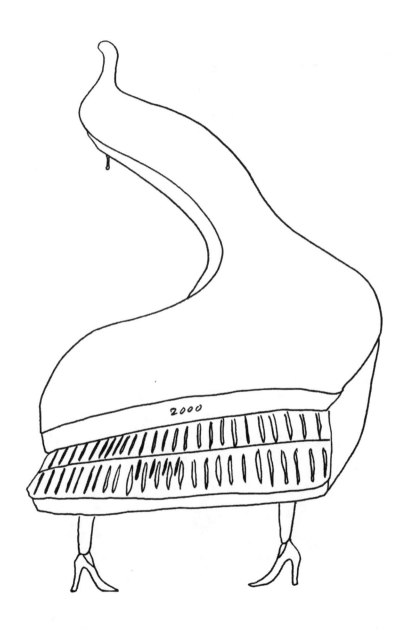

战争

下午的太阳宽容地依在墓碑上
一个低沉的声音缓缓地叙述着
瘦长的人们摘下军帽
遥远的生前，村里住满亲人……

WAR

The afternoon sun leans charitably over the headstone
A low deep voice slowly narrates
Tall thin people doff their army caps
Distant lives, a village full of kin…

1972

黄昏

寂寞潜潜地苏醒
细节也在悄悄进行
诗人抽搐着，产下
甲虫般无人知晓的感觉
——在照例被佣人破坏的黄昏……

DUSK

Loneliness secretly revives
Details also stealthily advance
The poet twitches, Gives birth
Like a beetle to unknown feelings
— In a dusk disrupted as usual by hired servants

1973

夜

在充满象征的夜里
月亮象病人苍白的脸
象一个错误的移动的时间
而死，象一个医生站在床前：

一些无情的感情
一些心中可怕的变动
月光在屋前的空场上轻声咳嗽
月光，暗示着楚楚在目的流放……

NIGHT

On a night full of symbols
The moon is like an invalid's pallid face
Like a mistaken shifted time
And death, like a doctor standing before the bed:

Some merciless emotions
Some internally chilling changes
Moonlight in the void before the room softly coughs
Moonlight hinting clearly at exile in the eye...

1973

解放

革命者在握紧的拳头上睡去
"解放"慢慢在他的记忆中成熟
像不眠的梦，像一只孤独的帆角
爱情也不再知道它的去处
只有上帝在保佑它惊心动魄的归宿……

LIBERATION

The revolutionary falls asleep on fists clenched tight
"Liberation" slowly ripens in his memory
Like a sleepless dream, like a solitary sail
Love too no longer knows where to go
There is only God to guard and bless its enthralling final abode…

1973

年代

沉闷的年代苏醒了
炮声微微地憾动大地
战争，在倔强地开垦
牲畜被征用，农民从田野上归来
抬着血淋淋的犁……

ERA

An oppressive era has revived
The sound of gunfire faintly shakes the earth
War, stubbornly reclaims the land
Livestock is requisitioned, peasants return from the fields
Toting ploughs dripping with blood

1973

海

海，向傍晚退去
带走了历史，也带走了哀怨
海，沉默着
不愿再宽恕人们，也不愿
再听到人们的赞美……

SEA

The sea, towards nightfall retreating
Carries off history, and carries off sadness
The sea, silent
Not wishing to pardon people again, nor
Hear people's praise again…

1973

致情敌

在自由的十字架上射死父亲
你怯懦的手第一次写下：叛逆
当你又从末日向春天走来
复活的路上横着你用旧的尸体

怀着血不会在荣誉上凝固的激动
我扶在巨人铜像上昏昏睡去
梦见在真理的冬天：
有我，默默赶开墓地上空的乌鸦……

TO THE RIVAL

On the cross of freedom shoot dead the father
For the first time your timorous hand writes: rebel
When again you walk over from doomsday to springtime
Your worn out corpse lies across the road to resurrection

Nurturing an excitement blood cannot congeal in glory
Drowsing over the bronze statue of the giant I fall asleep
Dream of me in the winter of truth:
Silently driving away the crows above the graveyard...

1973

致太阳

给我们家庭，给我们格言
你让所有的孩子骑上父亲肩膀
给我们光明，给我们羞愧
你让狗跟在诗人后面流浪

给我们时间，让我们劳动
你在黑夜中长睡，枕着我们的希望
给我们洗礼，让我们信仰
我们在你的祝福下，出生然后死亡

查看和平的梦境、笑脸
你是上帝的大臣
没收人间的贪婪、嫉妒
你是灵魂的君王

热爱名誉，你鼓励我们勇敢
抚摸每个人的头，你尊重平凡
你创造，从东方升起
你不自由，像一枚四海通用的钱！

TO THE SUN

Giving us family, giving us maxims
You make all the children ride on father's shoulders
Giving us light, giving us shame
You make dogs wander after poets

Giving us time, making us labor
You sleep long in the dark night, drowning our hopes
Giving us baptism, making us believe
We with your blessing, are born then die

Examining the peaceful dreamland, smiling faces
You are God's minister
Never having suffered human greed, envy
You are lord of the soul

Adoring fame, you encourage us to be brave
Caressing all our heads, you value the ordinary
You create, rise in the east
You are unfree, like a universally circulating coin!

1973

在秋天

秋天，米黄色的洋楼下
一个法国老太婆，死去了，慢慢地
在离祖国很远很远的地方
跑来了孩子们，一起，牵走她身旁的狗

把它的脖子系住，把它吊上白桦树
在离主人尸体不远的地方
慢慢地，死去了
一只纯种的法蓝西狗

在变得陌生的土地上
是这些孩子，这些分吃过老太婆糖果的孩子
一起，牵走她身旁的狗
把它吊上高高的白桦树

一起，死去了，慢慢地
一个法国老太婆，一只纯种的法蓝西狗
一些孩子们，一些中国的孩子们
在米黄色的洋楼下，在秋天……

IN AUTUMN

Autumn, in front of a cream-colored Western house
An old French woman, died, slowly
In a place far, far away from her homeland
Children who came running together, led away her faithful dog

Tied a rope around its neck, hung it from a white birch
In a place not far from the corpse of its mistress
Slowly, it died
A pedigree French dog

On earth turned unfamiliar
It was these children, who shared out the old woman's candies
Who together, led away her faithful dog
And hung it from a tall white birch

Together, they died, slowly
An old French woman, a pedigree French dog
Some children, some Chinese children
In front of a cream-colored Western house, in autumn…

1973

手艺

——和玛琳娜·茨维塔耶娃

　我写青春沦落的诗
（写不贞的诗）
写在窄长的房间中
被诗人奸污
被咖啡馆辞退街头的诗
我那冷漠的
再无怨恨的诗
（本身就是一个故事）
我那没有人读的诗
正如一个故事的历史
我那失去骄傲
失去爱情的
（我那贵族的诗）
她，终会被农民娶走
她，就是我荒废的时日……

HANDICRAFT

After Marina Tsvetaeva

I write youthful base poetry
(unchaste poetry)
Writing in a long narrow room
Raped by poets
This street corner poetry dismissed by the cafés
That cold
Now hateless poetry of mine
(itself a story)
My poetry read by no-one
Just like the history of a story
Now stripped of pride
Stripped of love
(That aristocratic poetry of mine)
She, will end up wed to a peasant
She, is my wasted days…

1973

诗人之死

是我死去的时候了
同一块土地，同一块天空
连同我一道，都那样寂静
呵，寂静，那样寂静
象在梦中一样，月光又高贵又无情
思想，大概已经停止
已不再有力量，答谢轻浮的生命
呵，寂静，那样温柔的寂静
生命轻轻飞去，象一阵离别的小风……

呵，寂静，那样寂静
象在梦中一样，月光又高贵又无情
在同一个黄昏，在同一个黎明
听不到挽歌，也听不到钟声
灵魂的大门，在庄严地关闭
送我加入迎娶生命的殡列
索我归还往日的才能
呵，寂静，那样永恒的寂静
没有回答，也没有回声
只有幽灵的火把，照亮我的一生……

DEATH OF THE POET

It was the time when I died
The same patch of earth, the same patch of sky
Accompanying me, all with such silence
Ah, silence, that silence
As in a dream, the moonlight both lofty and heartless
Thought, has probably already ceased
No more will it be powerful, acknowledge frivolous life
Ah, silence, that so tender silence
Life softly flying away, like a breeze taking its leave

Ah, silence, that silence
As in a dream, the moonlight is both lofty and heartless
The same dusk, the same dawn
No elegy to be heard, no tolling of bells
The portal to the realm of departed souls, solemnly closes
Seeing me into the funeral cortege that marries me to life
Demanding I revert to the talent of bygone days
Ah, silence, that eternal silence
There is no answer, there is no echo
Just the torches of ghosts, illuminating my whole life…

1974

教诲

只在一夜之间，伤口就挣开了
书架上的书籍也全部背叛了他们
只有当代最伟大的歌者
用弄哑的嗓音，俯在耳边，低声唱：
　　爵士的夜　　世纪的夜
他们已被高级的社会丛林所排除
并受限于这样的主题：
仅仅是为了衬托世界的悲惨
而出现的，悲惨
就成了他们一生的义务

谁说他们早期生活的主题
是明朗的，至今他们仍以为
那是一句有害的名言
在毫无艺术情节的夜晚
那灯光来源于错觉
他们所看到的永远是
一条单调的出现在冬天的坠雪的绳
他们只好不倦地游戏下去
和逃走的东西搏斗，并和
无从记忆的东西生活在一起
即使恢复了最初的憧憬
空虚，已成为他们一生的污点

INSTRUCTION

In memory of the dispirited

Just in the space of a night, the wound broke open
Even the books on the shelves all forsook them
There is only the current most magnificent singer
Singing softly, in a hoarse voice, into an ear:
   Night of a noble, night of a century
They have already been eliminated by the jungle of high society
And confined within a motif such as this:
They were merely deployed to highlight
The misery of the world, misery
Has become their lifelong duty

Who says that the motif of their early life
Was bright and cheerful, even now they think
That is a pernicious saying
In an evening with a totally artless plot
The lamplight has its source in illusion
All they ever see is
A monotonous rope that appears in the winter snowfall
They might as well carry on playing tirelessly
Struggle with elusive things, and
Live together with unmemorable things
If the earliest yearnings are revived
Emptiness, will be their lifelong stain

他们的不幸，来自理想的不幸
但他们的痛苦却是自取的
自觉，让他们的思想变得尖锐
并由于自觉而失血
但他们不能与传统和解
虽然在他们诞生之前
世界早已不洁地存在很久了
他们却仍要找到
第一个发现"真理"的罪犯
以及拆毁世界
所需要等待的时间

面对悬在颈上的枷锁
他们唯一的疯狂行为
就是拉紧它们
但他们不是同志
他们分散的破坏力重
还远远没有夺走社会的注意力
而仅仅沦为精神的犯罪者
仅仅因为：他们滥用了寓言

但最终，他们将在思想的课室中祈祷
并在看清自己笔迹的时候昏迷：
他们没有在主安排的时间内生活
他们是误生的人，在误解人生的地点停留
他们所经历的——仅仅是出生的悲剧

Their misfortune, comes from idealistic misfortune
But their suffering is brought on by themselves
It is awareness that sharpens their thinking
And through awareness blood is lost.
But they cannot grant traditional reconciliation
Although before their birth
The world had existed uncleanly for ages
They still want to find
The first culprit to discover 'truth'
And how long they must wait for
The destruction of the world

Given the nooses around their necks
Their only madness
Is to pull them tighter
But they are not comrades
Their scattered destructive strength
Still remote, has not seized the attention of society
And they are reduced to wrongdoers of the mind
Merely because: They misused parables.

But at the very end, they pray in the classroom of thought
And, when they see clearly their own writings, are stupefied:
They haven't lived in the Lord's arranged time
They are people who have missed life, stuck in a place where life is
       misunderstood
Everything they have gone through —— is a mere tragedy of birth

1976

那是我们不能攀登的大石

那是我们不能攀登的大石
为了造出它
我们议论了六年
我们造出它又向上攀登
你说大约还要七年
大约还要八年
一个更长的时间
还来得及得一次阑尾炎
手术进行了十年
好像刀光
一闪——

THE BIG ROCK WE CANNOT CLIMB

That's the big rock we cannot climb
To make it
We debated six years
We made it then climbed upwards
You said it probably needed seven years more
Probably another eight
Or a longer time
Time enough for an appendicitis
The operation took ten years
It was just like the flash of a knife ——

1982

妄想是真实的主人

而我们，是嘴唇贴着嘴唇的鸟儿
在时间的故事中
与人
进行最后一次划分：

钥匙在耳朵里扭了一下
影子已脱离我们
钥匙不停地扭下去
鸟儿已降低为人
鸟儿一无相识的人。

WISHFUL THINKING IS THE MASTER OF REALITY

And we, are birds beak to beak
In time's story
For the last time realizing our distinction
From people:

The key is turned in the ear
Shadows have broken away from us
The key keeps on turning
We have degenerated into people
We have become unrecognizable people

1982

噢怕，我怕

噢怕，我怕
什么?是我在问你
——你怕么?
是我在问自己。

判断是可怕的
敌人

我没有敌人。可我
更怕。假使夜
是一块巨大的桔皮
而枯肉在我嘴里
我怕——这是可能的

这是可能的。你怕么?
我的脸是透明的，其中有你
在看我。我俩互相看着
肉芽在同一张脸上迅速生长

除非瞎了，就要一直
看——互相看
在一杯漆黑的奶里
看。除非瞎了。瞎了

FEAR

Oh fear, I fear
What? I'm asking you.
—— What do you fear?
I'm asking myself.

Judgment is a fearful
Enemy

I have no enemy. But I
Fear even more. If night
Were a huge orange peel
And the pulp of the orange between my lips
I'd fear — this is possible

This is possible. What do you fear?
My face is transparent, within it is you
Looking at me. We look at each other
Sprouts of flesh growing rapidly on the same shared face

Unless blind, just keep on
Looking —— looking at each other
In a glass of pitch black milk
Look. Unless blind. Blind.

我更怕——被
一个简单的护士
缝着，在一张移植他人
眼睛的手术单下
会露出两个孩子的头

一个叫
或是一同叫
我都怕。想想都怕：

从打碎的窗子里拔出
我只有
一颗插满玻璃碴的头
还有两只可憎的手
会卡在棺盖外
而那是你的。我
不愿去想

从一颗树的上半截
锯下我
的下半截，而你疼着
叫着，你在叫：

我不再害怕。不疼
我并不疼，也跟着叫：
噢是的，你不再害怕。

I fear even more — when by
A simple nurse
I am being sewn up, under the operating sheet
In a transplant of another's eyes
May appear the heads of two children

One calls out
Or they call out together
I fear both. The mere thought I fear:
Pulled out of the smashed window
I have only
A head covered in shards of glass
And two abhorrent hands
To fix on the coffin lid
But they are yours. I
Don't want to think on it.

From the top half of a tree
Saw off my
Bottom half, and you are in pain
Shouting, you are shouting:
I fear no more. No pain
I have no pain at all, and carry on shouting:
Oh, yes, you fear no more.

1983

告别

长久地搂抱着白桦树
就像搂抱着我自己：
　　满山的红辣椒都在激动我
　　满手的石子洒向大地
　　满树，都是我的回忆……

秋天是一架最悲凉的琴
往事，在用力地弹着：
　　田野收割了
　　无家可归的叨野呵
　　如果你要哭泣，不要错过这大好时机！

FAREWELL

Forever embracing the white birch
Is just like embracing myself:
    a whole mountainful of red peppers stirring me
    a whole handful of pebbles scattered on the ground
    a whole tree, all of these are my memories…

Autumn is the most desolate of lutes
Things from the past, vigorously strumming:
    fields harvested
    ah, fields with no home to return to
    should you wish to cry, don't miss this big opportunity!

1983

死了。死了十头

又多了十头。多了
十头狮子

死后的事情：不多
也不少——刚好

剩下十条僵硬的
舌头。很像五双

变形的木拖鞋
已经生锈

的十根尾巴呵
很象十名兽医助手

手中的十根绳子
松开了。张开了

作梦的二十张眼皮：
在一只澡盆里坐着

十头狮子，哑了
但是活着。但是死了

DEAD, TEN DEAD

Another ten. Another
Ten lions

Things after death: not many
But not a few — happen to

Leave over ten stiff
Tongues. Very much like five pairs of

Deformed wooden shoes
Already rusted

Ten tails
Very much like ten veterinary assistants' hands

With ten ropes
Slackening. Opening

Twenty dreamy eyelids
Sitting in a bathtub

Ten lions, dumb
But alive. Yet dead

—— they're ten lions
Who starved a story

——是十头狮子
把一个故事

饿死了。故事
来自讲故事

的十只
多事的喉咙。

To death. Stories
Come from ten

Meddlesome throats
That tell stories

1983

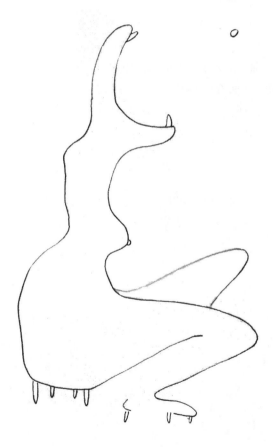

语言的制作来自厨房

要是语盲的制作来自厨房
内心就是卧室。他们说
内心要是卧室
妄想，就是卧室的主人

从鸟儿眼睛表达过的妄想里
摆弄弱音器的男孩子
承认：骚动
正像韵律

不会作梦的脑子
只是一块时间的荒地
摆弄弱音器的男孩子承认
但不懂得：

被避孕的种籽
并不生产形象
每一粒种籽是一个原因……
想要说出的

原因，正像地址
不说。抽烟的野蛮人
不说就把核桃
按进桌面，他们说

LANGUAGE IS MADE IN THE KITCHEN

If language is made in the kitchen
The heart is the bedroom. They say
If the heart is the bedroom
Wishful thinking is its master

From the wishful thinking expressed in the bird's eyes
The boy who fiddles with the trumpet mute
Agrees: commotion
Is just like meter

A brain incapable of dream
Is just a stretch of time's wasteland
The boy who fiddles with the mute recognizes
But does not understand

Contracepted seed
Just cannot produce images
Each seed is a reason…
Wanting to speak

A reason, just like an address
Does not speak. The wild man smoking a cigarette
Does not speak just presses the walnut
Into the table top. They speak

一切一切议论
应当停止——当
四周的马匹是那样安静
当它们，在观察人的眼睛……

Saying all discussion
Must cease — when
Horses all around are so silent
When they, are inspecting people's eyes

1983

醒来

窗外天空洁净呀
匣内思想辉煌

一百年内才摇一次头
一千年内才见一回面
红砖墙上的笔迹类似寓言
洁净的嘴唇洁净的语言

快　　好好地好好地
贴一下我们的脸
就贴那么一会儿时间
洁净的嘴唇洁净的睡眠

枯叶落地　　伤痕变紫
原来都是一种记忆
我们啊　　接受唯一的赐予
洁净的睡眠洁净的语言

别招唤　　就会到来
欲望原是金黄的谷粒
听我说　　唯一的唯一的
洁净的语言洁净的语言

WAKE UP

Outside the window the sky is clean
Inside the box thoughts sparkle

Only once in a hundred years a nod of the head
Only once in a thousand years an encounter
The writing on the red brick wall is like an allegory
Clean lips clean language

Quick   tightly tightly
Bring our faces together for a moment
Just for a short while
Clean lips clean sleep

Withered leaves fall to the ground   scars turn purple
Originally it was all a single memory
Oh we   received the only favor
Clean sleep clean language

Don't call out   it will come
Desire formerly was a golden grain
Listen to me   all there is, all there is
Clean language clean language

1983

从死亡的方向看

从死亡的方向看总会看到
一生不应见到的人
总会随便地埋到一个地点
随便嗅嗅，就把自己埋在那里
埋在让他们恨的地点

他们把铲中的土倒在你脸上
要谢谢他们。再谢一次
你的眼睛就再也看不到敌人
就会从死亡的方向传来
他们陷入敌意时的叫喊
你却再也听不见
那完全是痛苦的叫喊！

LOOKING OUT FROM DEATH

Looking out from death you will always see
Those whom all your life you ought not to see
You can always be buried somewhere as you please
Sniff around as you please, then bury yourself there
In a place that makes them hate

They shovel dirt in your face
You should thank them. And thank them again
Your eyes will never again see your enemy
Then from death will come
When they are consumed by enmity, a scream
Although you will never be able to hear again
Now that is the absolute scream of anguish!

1983

一个故事中有他全部的过去

当他敞开遍身朝向大海的窗户
向一万把钢刀碰响的声音投去
一个故事中有他全部的过去
当所有的舌头都向这个声音伸去
并且衔回了碰响这个声音的一万把钢刀
所有的日子都挤进一个日子
因此，每一年都多了一天

最后一年就翻倒在大橡树下
他的记忆来自一处牛栏，上空有一柱不散的烟
一些着火的儿童正拉着手围着厨刀歌唱
火焰在未熄灭之前
一直都在树上滚动燃烧
火焰，竟残害了他的肺

而他的眼睛是两座敌对城市的节日
鼻孔是两只巨大的烟斗仰望天空
女人，在用爱情向他的脸疯狂射击
使他的嘴唇留有一个空隙
一刻，一列与死亡对开的列车将要通过
使他伸直的双臂间留有一个早晨
正把太阳的头按下去

A SINGLE STORY TELLS HIS ENTIRE PAST

When he opens up the windows of his body which give onto the ocean
And leaps towards the sound of thousands of clashing knives
A single story tells his entire past
When all tongues stretch towards this sound
And bite back the thousands of knives of this clashing sound
All days will squeeze into one day
Thus, each year will have an extra day

The last year flips over under the great oak
His memory comes from a cattle pen, overhead is a pillar of lingering smoke
Some children on fire holding hands sing and dance in a circle round
       the kitchen knife
Before the flames die down
They persistently rage round the tree
The flames, finally injuring his lungs

And his eyes are the festival days of two hostile towns
His nostrils two enormous tobacco pipes pointed at the sky
Women wildly shoot love at his face
Forcing his lips agape
Any moment, a train traveling in the opposite direction to death will pass by
Forcing a morning between his outstretched arms
Pressing down the sun's head

一管无声手枪宣布了这个早晨的来临
一个比空盆子扣在地上还要冷淡的早晨
一阵树林内折断树枝的声响
一根折断的钟锤就搁在葬礼街卸下的旧门板上
一个故事中有他全部的过去
死亡，已成为一次多余的心跳

当星星向寻找毒蛇毒液的大地飞速降临
时间，也在钟表的嘀嗒声外腐烂
耗子，在铜棺的锈斑上换牙
菌类，在腐败的地衣上跺着脚
蟋蟀的儿子在他身上长久地做针线
还有邪恶，在一面鼓上撕扯他的脸
他的体内已全部都是死亡的荣耀
全都都是，一个故事中有他全部的过去

一个故事中有他全部的过去
一个瘦长的男子正坐在截下的树墩上休息
第一次太阳这样近地阅读他的双眼
更近地太阳坐到他的膝上
太阳在他的指间冒烟
每夜我都手拿望远镜向那里瞄准
直至太阳熄灭的一刻
一个树墩在他坐过的地方休息

A silent revolver announces the approach of this morning
A morning more cheerless than an empty basin thrown to the ground
A sound of branches breaking in the forest
A broken pendulum on an old door shutter lifted down
       from the funereal street
A single story tells his entire past
Death, has become a superfluous beat of the heart

When stars dive towards the snake venom-seeking earth
Time, rots beyond the tick-tocking of the clock
Rats, shed their milk teeth on the rust spots of the copper coffin
Fungi, stamp their feet on decaying lichen
The son of the cricket does laborious needlework on his body
And then there is evil, tearing apart his face on a drum
His body now entirely filled with death's glory
Entirely, a single story tells his entire past

A single story tells his entire past
A thin lanky man sits resting on a tree stump
The first time the sun reads his eyes closely
And closer still it sits on his knees
The sun makes smoke between his fingers
Every night I fix my telescope on that spot
Until the moment the sun dies out
A tree stump takes its rest where he sat

比五月的白菜畦还要寂静
他赶的马在清晨走过
死亡，已碎成一堆纯粹的玻璃
太阳已变成一个滚动在送葬人回家路上的雷
而孩子细嫩的脚丫正走上常绿的橄榄枝
而我的头肿大着，像千万只马蹄在击鼓
与粗大的弯刀相比，死亡只是一粒沙子
所以一个故事中有他全都的过去
所以一千年也扭过脸来——看

More silent than a cabbage patch in May
The horse he rode walks past in the early morning
Death, has fragmented into a mound of pure glass
The sun has become the thunder rolling down the road
       of the mourners returning home
And the children's slender feet tiptoe onto evergreen olive branches
And my head swells up, like millions of horse hooves stamping on drums
Compared to big, crude, curved knives, death is but a grain of sand
So a single story tells his entire life
So a thousand years turn away their face — look

1983

病人

三年前乐音停止
空指环划过玻璃表面
一小块儿天空
从窗上裁下
讲话

但不再发出声音
话语在窗外散开
看它们它们就变成苹果
声音浸透了果肉
烟，老是想回到冒出它们的地方

三年来在坑里
我栽下了树
有着很美很美面孔的人
常在树前站立

看到要讥笑我的人走来
落叶，就把坑覆盖……

THE PATIENT

Three years ago the music stopped
Freed fingers drew circles on a glass surface
A small patch of sky
Cut out by the window
Talked

But no longer emitted sound
Words dispersed outside the window
Looking at them they turned into apples
Sounds slowly penetrated fruit
Smoke, always wants to return to the place they came from

For three years down in a pit
I have planted trees
People with beautiful, beautiful faces
Often standing before the trees

Seeing people wanting to sneer at me come over
Falling leaves, cover the pit...

1984

北方的海

北方的海，巨型玻璃混在冰中汹涌
一种寂寞，海兽发现大陆之前的寂寞
土地呵，可曾知道取走天空意味着什么

在运送猛虎过海的夜晚
一只老虎的影子从我脸上经过
——噢，我吐露我的生活

而我的生命没有任何激动。没有
我的生命没有人与人交换血液的激动
如我不能占有一种记忆——比风还要强大

我会说：这大海也越来越旧了
如我不能依靠听力——那消灭声音的东西
如我不能研究笑声

——那期待着从大海归来的东西
我会说：靠同我身体同样渺小的比例
我无法激动

但是天以外的什么引得我的注意：
石头下蛋，现实的影子移动
在竖起来的海底，大海日夜奔流

NORTHERN SEA

Northern sea, giant glass crashing haphazardly in ice
A loneliness, the loneliness preceding the sea creatures' discovery of land
Oh earth, could you have known what taking away the sky implied

The night when wild tigers were shipped across the sea
A tiger's shadow passed over my face
— Oh, I'm spurting out my life

But there is no excitement in my life. None
In my life there is no excitement of people exchanging blood
If I cannot possess a memory — stronger than the wind

I'll say: This ocean also gets older
If I cannot rely on my hearing — that thing that extinguishes sound
If I cannot study the sound of laughter

— Then awaiting the thing that returns from the ocean
I'll say: Things of a scale as insignificant as my body
Cannot excite me

But what lies beyond the sky attracts my attention
A stone lays an egg, reality's shadow shifts
Upon the seabed stood erect, the ocean gushes onward night and day

——初次呵，我有了喜悦
这些都是我不曾见过的
绸子般的河面，河流是一座座桥梁

绸子抖动河面，河流在天上疾滚
一切物象让我感动
并且奇怪喜悦，在我心中有了陌生的作用

在这并不比平时更多地拥有时间的时刻
我听到蚌，在相爱时刻
张开双壳的声响

多情人流泪的时刻——我注意到
风暴掀起大地的四角
大地有着被狼吃掉最后一个孩子后的寂静

但是从一只高高升起的大篮子中
我看到所有爱过我的人们
是这样紧紧地紧紧地紧紧地——搂在一起……

— The first time, I knew happiness:
These are what I haven't seen
Silk-like river surface, the river is a bridge

Silk shaking the river surface, the river crashing about in the sky
All phenomena of nature move me
And odd happiness, in my mind have a strange deployment

In this moment when I possess time no more than usual
I hear oysters, at the moment of making love
The sound of their shells opening

At the moment when many lovers weep — I notice
The storm lifts up the four corners of the earth
A silence which follows the last child's being devoured by wolves
covers the earth

But from a large basket lifted up high
I see all those who have loved me
Closely, closely, closely — huddled together...

1984

是

是　黎明在天边糟蹋的
一块多好的料子
是黑夜与白昼
互相占有的时刻
是曙光　从残缺的金属大墙背后
露出的残废的　脸
　　我爱你
　　我永不收回去

是　炉子倾斜　太阳崩溃在山脊
孤独奔向地裂
是风
一个盲人邮差　走入地心深处
它绿色的血
抹去了一切声音　我信
它带走的字：
　　我爱你
　　我永不收回去

是昔日的歌声　一串瞪着眼睛的铃铛
是河水的镣拷声
打着小鼓
是你的蓝眼睛　两个太阳
从天而降
　　我爱你
　　我永不收回去

IT'S

It's   a piece of fine cloth
Trampled on the horizon by dawn
It's the moment night and day
Invade each other
It's daybreak   through the corroded big metal wall
Exposed mutilated   faces
    I love you
    I shall never take it back

It's   the stove slanting   the sun slumping on the mountain ridge
Loneliness rushing towards the crack in the earth
It's the wind
A blind postman walking deep into the earth's core
Its green-colored blood
Has wiped away all sound   I believe
The words it carried away:
    I love you
    I shall never take it back

It's the song of the days gone by   a string of bells with glaring eyes
It's the sound of the river's fetters
Beating small drums
It's the two suns of your blue eyes
Fallen from the sky
    I love you
    I shall never take it back

是两把锤子　　轮流击打
来自同一个梦中的火光
是月亮　　重如一粒子弹
把我们坐过的船　　压沉
是睫毛膏　　永恒地贴住
　　我爱你
　　我永不收回去

是失去的一切
肿胀成河流
是火焰　　火焰是另一条河流
火焰　　永恒的钩子
钩爪全都向上翘起
是火焰的形状
碎裂　　碎在星形的
伸出去　　而继续燃烧的手指上　　是
　　我爱你
　　我永不收回去

It's two hammers   taking turns to strike
Flames from the one dream
It's moonlight   heavy as a bullet
Sinking the boat we'd sailed in
It's the mascara   perpetually applied
   I love you
   I shall never take it back

It's all that is lost
Swelling into a river
It's flames   flames are another river
Flames   perpetual hooks:
Claws all pointing upwards
It's the shape of the flames
Splintering   splintering over star-shaped
Out-stretched   and still burning fingers   It's
   I love you
   I shall never take it back

1985

里 程

一条大路吸引令你头晕的最初的方向
那是你的起点。云朵包住你的头
准备给你一个工作
那是你的起点
那是你的起点
当监狱把它的性格塞进一座城市
砖石在街心把你搂紧
每年的大雪是你的旧上衣
天空，却总是一所蓝色的大学

天空，那样惨白的天空
刚刚被拧过脸的天空
同意你笑，你的胡子
在匆忙地吃饭
当你追赶穿越时间的大树
金色的过水的耗子，把你梦见：
你是强大的风暴中一粒卷曲的蚕豆
你是一把椅子，属于大海
要你在人类的海边，从头读书

寻找自己，在认识自己的旅程中
北方的大雪，就是你的道路
肩膀上的肉，就是你的粮食
头也不回的旅行者啊
你所蔑视的一切，都是不会消逝的

MILESTONES

A main road attracts the very first direction that makes you dizzy
That is your starting point. Clouds envelop your head
Preparing to give you a job
That is your starting point
That is your starting point
When the jail squeezes its temperament into a city
Bricks and stones in the middle of the road hold you tight
Every year's snowfall is your old jacket
The sky, however is always a blue university

The sky, that miserably pale sky
Sky whose face has just been pinched
Agrees to your smile, your beard
Hastily eating
When you pursue the big tree that penetrates time
Golden rats having crossed the water, dream of you:
You are a crinkled bean in a fierce storm
You are a chair, belonging to the ocean
Wanting you on the shore of humanity, to study all over again

To seek yourself, on the journey when you know yourself
Northern snow, that's your road
Flesh on shoulders, that's your food
Oh traveler you who do not even look back
Of everything you hold in contempt, nothing will ever vanish

1985

灌木

我们反复说过的话它们听不见
它们彼此看也不看
表面上看也不看
根

却在泥土中互相寻找
找到了就扭杀
我们中间有人把
这种行为称为：
爱

刚从树丛中爬起来的恋人
也在想这件事儿
他们管它叫：
做爱。

SHRUBS

What we've said over and over they can't hear
They see each other but do not see
On the surface see but do not see
Roots

However seek each other in the mud
Once found they twist each other to death
Amongst us there are people who
Call this behavior:
Love

Lovers who have just climbed trees
Are also thinking this over
They call it:
Making love.

1985

走路

出于迟迟没有到达的原因
你们朝前走
只要一走
只要一走
就永远不会到达了
你们知道你们知道
而你们走去
在一个倒置的箱子里
头朝下地走那箱子的顶
走到一直走到
脚踩住手的时候

你们用最笨的办法走过这城市

WALKING

Because you are so late in arriving
You people go forward
Just setting out
Just setting out
But never able to arrive
You know you know
But you go on
In an upturned box
Head down you advance on the lid of the box
Walking on and on until
Your feet tread on your hands

You walk through this city in the most stupid fashion

1985

哑孩子

那男人的眼睛从你脸上
往外瞪着瞪着那女人
抓着墙壁抓着它的脸
用了生下一个孩子的时间
你的小模样
就从扇贝的卧室中伸出来了
那两扇肉门红扑扑的
而你的身体
是锯

暴力摇撼着果树
哑孩子把头藏起
口吃的情欲玫瑰色的腋臭
留在色情的棺底
肉作的绸子水母的皮肤
被拉成一只长筒丝袜的哀号
哑孩子喝着喝着整个冬天的愤怒：
整夜那男人烦躁地撕纸
整夜他骂她是个死鬼！

DUMB CHILD

That man's eyes staring out of your face
Staring at that woman
Clutching the wall clutching its face
In the time it takes to give birth to a child
Your little shape
Protrudes from the shell-like bedroom
Those two flesh doors throbbing red
And your body
Are saws

Violently shaking fruit trees
The dumb child hides its head
Stuttered lust, the odor of rose-colored armpits
Lingers under the pornographic coffin
Silk made of flesh jellyfish skin
Pulled into the wail of a long silk stocking
Dumb child shouting shouting a whole winter's anger
All night long excitedly that man tears paper
All night long calls her a demon!

1986

关怀

早晨，一阵鸟儿肚子里的说话声
把母亲惊醒。醒前（一只血枕头上画着田野怎样入睡）
鸟儿，树权翘起的一根小姆指
鸟儿的头，一把金光闪闪的小凿子
嘴，一道铲形的光
翻动着藏于地层中的蛹：
"来，让我们一同种植
　　　世界的关怀！"

鸟儿用童声歌唱着
用顽固的头研究一粒果核
（里面包着永恒的饥饿）
这张十六岁的鸟儿脸上
两只恐怖的黑眼圈
是一只倒置的望远镜
从中射来粒粒粗笨的猎人
——群摇摇晃晃的大学生
背包上写着：永恒的寂寞。

从指缝中察看世界，母亲
就在这时把头发锁入柜中
一道难看的闪电扭歪了她的脸
（类似年轮在树木体内沉思的图景）
大雪，摇着千万只白手

SOLICITUDE

Early morning, the sound of talking in the bird's stomach
Startles the mother awake. Before awaking (on a bloody pillow
Is drawn: how fields fall asleep)
The bird, a little thumb sticking out from a branch
The bird's head, a little golden glistening chisel
Its beak, a trowel-shaped ray of light
Turns over lava hidden in the layers of earth
"Come let's plant together
    The world's solicitude!"

The bird sings with unbroken voice
Studies a kernel with a stubborn head
(Wrapped inside is perpetual hunger)
In this sixteen-year-old bird face
Two terrifying black eye sockets
Are a pair of inverted binoculars
From which pellet-like are shot ungainly hunters
—— a crowd of swaying students
And written on their knapsacks: perpetually lonely.

Inspecting the world through finger cracks, mother
At just this moment locks her hair in the cabinet
A flash of ugly lightning twists her face
(like the prospect of annual rings pondering in a tree trunk)
Snow, shaking millions of hands

正在降下，雪道上
两行歪歪斜斜的足迹
一个矮子像一件黑大衣
正把骯脏的田野走得心烦意乱……

于是，猛地，从核桃的地层中
从一片麦地
我认出了自己的内心：
一阵血液的愚蠢的激流
一阵牛奶似的抚摸
我喝下了这个早晨
我，在这个早晨来临。

Falling, on the snowy path
Two lines of crooked footprints
A dwarf looking like a black overcoat
Is walking through filthy fields annoying them to distraction…

Then, suddenly, from layers of walnuts
From a wheat field
I recognize my own inner mind:
A bloody, foolish torrent
A milky embrace
I drank down this morning
This morning, I came near.

1986

风车

永恒的轮子到处转着
我是那不转的
像个颓废的建筑瘫痪在田野
我，在向往狂风的来临：

那些比疼痛还要严重的
正在隆隆走来，统治我的头顶
雷电在天空疾驰着编织
天空如石块，在崩溃后幻想
尾巴在屁股上忙乱着
牛羊，挤成一堆逃走
就是这些东西，堆成了记忆
让我重把黑暗的呼啸
搂向自己……

而，我们的厄运，我们的主人
站在肉做的田野的尽头
用可怕的脸色，为风暴继续鼓掌——

WINDMILL

Perpetual wheels turn on all sides
Yet I do not turn
Like a dejected edifice paralyzed in the fields
I, yearn for the advent of a fierce wind:

Those aches will be even more severe
Rumbling forth, governing my head
Thunder and lightning in the sky frantically weaving
The sky like a stone, fantasizing after collapsing
Tails on buttocks flail about
Cattle and sheep, piled into a heap flee
Precisely these things, heaped into memory
Make me once more hold to myself
The roar of darkness...

And, our bad fortune, our master
Standing at the head of the field made of flesh
With a terrifying expression, continues clapping for the storm —

1986

中选

一定是在早晨。镜中一无所有，你回身
旅馆单间的钥匙孔变为一只男人的假眼
你发出第一声叫喊

大海，就在那时钻入一只海蛎
于是，突然地，你发现，已经置身于
一个被时间砸开的故事中

孤独地而又并非独自地
用无知的信念喂养
一个男孩儿

在你肚子中的重量
呼吸，被切成了块儿
变成严格的定量

一些星星抱着尖锐的石头
开始用力舞蹈
它们酷似那男人的脸

而他要把它们翻译成自己未来的形象
于是，你再次发出一声叫喊
喊声引来了医生

CHOOSING

It is definitely in the morning. Absolutely nothing in the mirror,
        you turn round
The keyhole to the single hotel room becomes a man's glass eye
You let out your first scream

The ocean, just then bores through an oyster
Suddenly, you discover, you have already placed yourself in
A story smashed open by time

Solitary but there again not at all alone
With unknown beliefs nourishing
A boy

The weight in your stomach
Breathing, sliced into pieces
Becomes a rigidly fixed quantity

Some stars embracing sharp stones
Start to dance energetically
They are the very likeness of that man's face

And he wants to translate them into his future image
Then, you let out another scream
And the sound of screaming brings a doctor

耳朵上缠着白纱布
肩膀上挎着修剪婴儿睫毛的药械箱
埋伏在路旁的树木

也一同站起
最后的喊声是：
    "母亲青春的罪！"

Ears bound with white gauze
Arms bearing a box of medical instruments for trimming
infants' eyelashes.
Trees lying in ambush by the roadside

Also stand up together
The final scream is:
'Mother's sin of youth!'

1987

改造

用被改造的工具改造着语言
用被改造的语言—
继续改造着

每一代
都在这桌上乱摸一阵
恰好到了这上代

他
刚伸出手
女孩子们就开始笑

被他发觉了
陪着她们一同笑
直至变为更加可笑：

他刚伸出手
水流就中断
他把手移开

水流，也不再流……

REFASHIONING

With refashioned tools refashion language
With refashioned language
Continue to refashion

Every generation
Paws over this table
And then this generation happens along

He
Just stretches out a hand
And girls start to laugh

When he realizes,
He laughs with them
Until he becomes even more laughable:

He just stretches out a hand
And the water stops flowing
He moves his hand

The water, does not flow again...

1987

1986 年 6 月 30 日

横跨太平洋我爱人从美国传信来
"那片麦子死了——连同麦地中央的墓地"

这是一种手法——等于
往一个男人屁股上多踢了一脚

就算盖了邮戳
一共 44 美分

这景象背后留有一道伏笔
譬如，曼哈顿一家鞋店门口有一幅标语

"我们来自不同的星球"
或者，一块从费城送往辛辛那提的

三种肤色的生日蛋糕上写的：
"用一个孩子愈合我们之间的距离"

这景象背后再无其它景象
惟一的景象是在旧金山：

从屁股兜里摸出
一块古老的东方的猪油肥皂

一个搀扶盲人过街的水手
把它丢进了轰鸣的宇宙。

JUNE 30, 1986

From America my lover sends a message straddling the Pacific:
"That wheat is dead — along with the burial ground at the center
     of the wheat field"

This is a trick — like
Kicking a man several times up the backside

It's no more than sticking on a stamp
Cost: 44 cents

On the back of this picture is a laconic note:
Such as, the slogan over the door of a Manhattan shoe shop:

"We come from different planets"
Or, sent from Philadelphia to Cincinnati, a piece of

Three skin-colored birthday cake, with the lettering:
"Heal the distance between us with a child"

On the back of this picture there is no other picture
The only picture is of San Francisco:

Rummaging out of a backside pocket
A lump of ancient oriental pig lard soap

A sailor helping a blind man cross the road
Tosses it into the raging universe.

1988

1988 年 2 月 11 日

纪念普拉斯

1

这住在狐皮大衣里的女人
是一块夹满发夹的云

她沉重的臀部，让以后的天空
有了被坐弯的屋顶的形状

一个没有了她的世界存有两个孩子
脖子上坠着奶瓶

已被绑上马背。他们的父亲
正向马腹狠踢临别的一脚；

"你哭，你喊，你止不住，你
就得用药!"

FEBRUARY 1988

In memory of Sylvia Plath

1

This woman who lived in an unsociable and eccentric overcoat
Is a cluster of cloud stuffed full of hairpins
Her heavy buttocks, give the sky that follows
The shape of a roof that's been sat on
In a world without her there are two children
Feeding bottles hung round their necks
Bound onto a horse's back. Their father
Directs a ruthless parting kick at the horse's belly;
'You cry, you scream, you cannot stop, you
should take something for it!'

2

用逃离眼窝的瞳仁追问："那列
装满被颠昏的苹果的火车，可是出了轨？"

黑树林毫无表情，代替风
阴沉的理性从中穿行

"用外省的口音招呼它们
它们就点头？" 天空的脸色

一种被辱骂后的痕迹
像希望一样

静止。"而我要吃带尖儿的东西！"
面对着火光着身子独坐的背影

一阵解毒似的圆号声———永不腐烂的神经
把她的理解啐向空中⋯⋯

2

With eyes jumping out of their sockets you ask minutely: "That
train packed full of shaken confused apples, was it derailed?"

The black forest is totally without expression, in place of the wind
Somber reason pierces through

"When you greet them with an out-of-town accent
do they nod?" The sky's expression

A mark left by insults
Is like hope

At a standstill. 'And I want to eat pointed things!'
Facing the shadow cast by firelight of the back of a body sat alone

An antidotary blast of French horn — an undecayable nerve
Spits her understanding into the sky...

1988

北方的土地

总是数着脉搏，目送河流远去
总是依着木桌，思念大雪
斧声和劈出木柴的蝗虫
总是在触到过冬的冻土，脚
就认定，我属于这里
我属于这里，我记录，我测量，我饲喂
仪器以生肉，我认定：这里，在这里
　　总是在这里——

在，一个石头国王背向阳光屹立的国度
在，一个大打麦场，一个空空的放假的教室
在，大雪从天空的最深处出发之前
五十朵坏云，经过摘棉人的头顶
一百个老女人，向天外飞去
一千个男孩子，站在天边撒尿
一亿个星球，继续荒凉着
一个世纪了——

祖先阴沈的脸色，遮暗了排排石像
石头们，在彼此的距离间安放
桦树林内，吊着件件黑呢大衣
麦穗上，系着收割妇的红头巾
　　季节，季节

NORTHERN EARTH

Always counting a pulse, watching a river fly into the distance
Always leaning on a wooden table, longing for heavy snow
The sound of an axe and the locusts splitting out of the firewood
Always when touching the wintered frozen soil, feet
Know for certain, I belong here
I belong here, I remember, I survey, I feed
Instruments with raw meat, I firmly believe:
       Being here, right here, always here ——

Being in, a country where a stone king stands erect with his back
       to the sun
Being in, a big threshing ground, in an empty classroom during
       the holidays
Being in, the snow before it leaves the deepest part of the sky
Fifty bad clouds roll above the heads of cotton-pickers
One hundred old women fly into outer space
One thousand boys urinate over the horizon,
One hundred million stars continue being desolate
One century goes by ——

Forbears with gloomy countenance, darken rows of statues
Stones, arranged at a distance from each other
In the pine forest, are draped in black woolen overcoats
To the heads of wheat are tied the red scarves of women reapers
       Seasons, seasons

用永不消逝的纪律
把我们种到历史要去的路上————
总是在这个季节，在多余的季节
冬天的阅读，放慢了，田野的书页
不再翻动，每个读书人的头，
都陷入了隐秘————得到公开后的激动：

  你的荒凉，枕在挖你的坑中
  你的记忆，已被挖走
  你的宽广，因为缺少哀愁，
  而枯槁，你，就是哀愁自身———

  你在哪里，哪里就有哀愁
从，那块失败的麦地的额角
七十亩玉米地，毁了你的脑子
更加广大的菜地，静寂无声
比草更弱的，你己不再能够听见
你要对自己说的，继续涌出：
  "那是你们的福音……"

With discipline that will never disappear
Plant us in the road that history wants to take —
Always in this season, in a superfluous season
Winter reading, goes slowly, the pages of the field
Are no longer turned, every reader's head
Falls into deep secrecy —— affected by the shock of opening up.
      Your desolation, lies in the holes being dug in you.
      Your memory, has been dug away,
      Your expanse, through a lack of sorrow
      Dries up, you, are sorrow itself ——

      Wherever you are, there will be sorrow
From, the temples of that defeated wheat field
Seventy *mu* of corn, destroy your brain
Widening vegetable plots, no sound at all
More feeble than the grass, already you can no longer hear
You want to say to yourself, continuously pour out:
      "That is your gospel…"

1988

九月

九月，盲人抚摸麦浪前行，养麦
发出寓言中的清香
— 二十年前的天空

滑过读书少年的侧影
开窗我就望见，树木伫立
背诵记忆：林中有一块空地

揉碎的花瓣纷纷散落
在主人的脸上找到了永恒的安息地
一阵催我鞠躬的旧风

九月的云朵，已变为肥堆
暴风雨到来前的阴暗，在处理天空
用擦泪的手巾遮着

母亲低首割草，众裁缝埋头工作
我在傍晚读过的书
再次化为黑沉沉的土地……

SEPTEMBER

In September, the blind advance caressing waves of wheat, stately wheat
Emits a fragrance born of parables
— the sky of twenty years past

Glides past the profile of a boy at study
Opening the window I contemplate, trees standing still
Reciting their memories: in the forest is an empty space

Petals rubbed to bits fall and scatter one after another
On the Lord's face finding a perpetual place of rest
A gust of old wind that makes me bow

September clouds, turned to compost heaps
The dark before the storm, handling the sky
Covering it with a tear-soaked handkerchief

Mother head bowed cuts the grass, tailors heads buried in their work
The books I studied as evening approached
Once more turn to black heavy earth...

1988

笨女儿

在漆黑的夜里为母亲染发，马蹄声
近了。母亲的棺材
开始为母亲穿衣
母亲的鞋，独自向树上爬去
留给母亲的风，像铁一样不肯散开
母亲的终结
意味着冬天
从仇恨中解体

冬天，已把它的压力完成
马蹄声，在响亮的铁板上开了花
在被雪擦亮的大地之上，风
说风残忍
意味着另一种残忍：说
逃向天空的东西
被麻痹在半空
意味着母亲的一生
只是十根脚趾同时折断
说母亲往火中投着木炭
就是投着孩子，意味着笨女儿
同情炉火中的灰烬
说这就是罪，意味着：
"我會再犯！"

STUPID GIRL

In the pitch black night dyeing mother's hair, the sound of horseshoes
Approaches. Mother's coffin
Starting to put on clothing for mother.
Mother's shoes, climb up the tree alone
Wind left for mother, like iron refuses to disperse
Mother's end
Means winter
Out of enmity disintegrates

Winter, has already completed its oppression
The sound of horse hooves, blossoms on the clanging iron plate
On the earth swept to glinting by the snow, the wind
Says the wind is cruel,
Meaning a different sort of cruelty: says
Things which escape into the sky,
Are paralyzed in mid-air,
Meaning mother's whole life
Is just ten toes simultaneously broken
Says mother throwing charcoal in the fire
Is throwing a child, meaning a stupid girl
Sympathizing with the ashes in the fire
Says this is wrong, meaning:
'I will offend again!'

1988

过程

一只成熟的柿子，墜落在半空
一只生锈的梨，已经搁到地上
地上的桔皮，已被一一拾走
　　它们剩下了你

　　这样的一个过程

先于梦，你到达了那里
先于你，有人从那里返回
先于你们，更多的人尚未出发
　　你跟随了他们

　　这样的一个过程

你用手捂住脸，手已退化成手套
手套上保留着指甲，把腿上的肉抓紧
你走向生活——可能得到延长的方向
　　上前一步，你凑到小便池边

　　你把这过程结束。

PROCESS

A ripe persimmon, falling in mid-air
A rusty pear, already fallen to earth
Orange peel on the ground, long since picked up bit by bit
   They left you over

  A process like this

Before dream, you arrive there
Before you, there are those who've long since returned from there
Before you people, even more people who have not yet set out
   You follow them

  A process like this

You cover your face with hands, hands degraded into gloves
The gloves having kept the fingernails, firmly grasp the leg's flesh
You walk towards life — maybe attain a prolonged course
   Another step forward, you happen on a piss-pond

  You conclude this process

1989

居民

他们在天空深处喝啤酒时，我们才接吻
他们歌唱时，我们熄灯
我们入睡时，他们用镀银的脚指甲
走进我们的梦，我们等待梦醒时

他们早已组成了河流

在没有时间的睡眠里
他们刮脸，我们就听到提琴声
他们划桨，地球就停转
他们不划，他们不划

我们就没有醒来的可能

在没有睡眠的时间里
他们向我们招手，我们向孩子招手
孩子们向孩子们招手时
星星们从一所遥远的旅馆中醒来了

一切会痛苦的都醒来了
他们喝过的啤酒，早已流回大海
那些在海面上行走的孩子
全都受到他们的祝福：流动

流动，也只是河流的屈从

用偷偷流出的眼泪，我们组成了河流……

RESIDENTS

When they drink beer in the depths of the sky, then we kiss
When they sing, we turn off the light
When we fall asleep, on silver-plated toenails
They walk into our dream, while we await the dream's end

They have long since formed a river

In timeless sleep
They shave, then we hear the sound of strings
They paddle their oars, then the world stops turning
They don't paddle, they don't paddle

Then we have no chance of awakening

In sleepless time
They wave to us, we wave to the children
When children wave to children
Stars awake from a distant hotel

All who feel pain will awaken

The beer they drank has long since flowed back to the ocean
Those children walking on the surface of the sea
All received their blessing: flowing

Flowing, is but the river's yielding

With secretly shed tears, we formed a river…

1989

阿姆斯特丹的河流

十一月入夜的城市
惟有阿姆斯特丹的河流

突然

我家树上的桔子
在秋风中晃动

我关上窗户，也没有用
河流倒流，也没有用
那镶满珍珠的太阳，升起来了

也没有用

鸽群像铁屑散落
没有男孩子的街道突然显得空阔

秋雨过后
那爬满蜗牛的屋顶
— 我的祖国

从阿姆斯特丹的河上，缓缓驶过……

THE RIVERS OF AMSTERDAM

November as the city enters night
There are only the rivers of Amsterdam

Suddenly

The mandarins on the tree at home
Quiver in the autumn breeze

I shut the window, yet to no avail
The rivers flow backwards, yet to no avail
That sun all inlaid with pearls, has risen

Yet to no avail

Doves like iron filings scatter and fall
A road devoid of boys suddenly looks vast and empty

After the passing of the autumn rain
That roof crawling with snails
— my motherland

On Amsterdam's rivers, slowly sailing by...

1989

走向冬天

树叶发出的声音，变了
腐烂的果核，刺痛路人的双眼

昔日晾晒谷粒的红房屋顶上
小虫精亮的尸首，堆积成秋天的内容

秋意，在准备过冬的呢大衣上刷着
菌类，已从朽坏的棺木上走向冬天

阳光下的少年，已变得丑陋
大理石父母，高声哭泣：

水在井下经过时
犁，已死在地里

铁在铁匠手中弯曲时
收割人把弯刀搂向自己怀中

结伴送葬的人醉得东摇西晃
五月麦浪的翻译声，已是这般久远

树木，望着准备把她们嫁走的远方
牛群，用憋住粪便的姿态抵制天穹的移动……

WALKING INTO WINTER

Sounds emitted by the leaves, have changed
Rotting fruit and kernels, sting the eyes of the passer-by

On the red roofs where the grain was sunned
Shimmering skulls of tiny insects, piled up as autumn's substance

A touch of autumn, is brushed from a woolen overcoat preparing
     for winter
Fungi, from decaying coffin wood have already walked into winter

Youngsters in sunlight, have become ugly
Marble parents, sob noisily:

When water at the well-bottom is gone
Ploughs, are dead in the ground

When the iron is bent in the smithy's hands
The harvesters hold bent blades to their breasts

Those in the funeral procession are rolling drunk
The translated sounds of the wheat waves of May, are already so remote

Trees, contemplate the faraway places preparing to marry them off
Cows, in bowel-tightening dung-retaining posture defy the movement
     of the heavens…

1989

在英格兰

当教堂的尖顶与城市的烟囱沉下地平线后
英格兰的天空，比情人的低语声还要阴暗
两个盲人手风琴演奏者，垂首走过

没有农夫，便不会有晚祷
没有墓碑，便不会有朗诵者
两行新栽的苹果树，刺痛我的心

是我的翅膀使我出名，是英格兰
使我到达我被失去的地点
记忆，但不再留下犁沟

耻辱，那是我的地址
整个英格兰，没有一个女人不会亲嘴
整个英格兰，容不下我的骄傲

从指甲缝中隐藏的泥土，我
认出我的祖國——母亲
已被打进一个小包裹，远远寄走……

IN ENGLAND

After the church spires and the city chimneys sink beneath the horizon
England's sky, is darker than lovers' whispers
Two blind accordion players, heads bowed pass by

There are no farmers, so there are no vespers
There are no tombstones, so there are no declaimers
Two rows of newly planted apple trees, stab my heart

It was my wings that brought me fame, it was England
Brought me to the place where I was lost
Memories, but no longer leaving furrows

Shame, that's my address
The whole of England, does not possess a woman who cannot kiss
The whole of England, cannot contain my pride

From the mud hidden in the cracks of my nails, I
Recognize my homeland — mother
Stuffed into a parcel, and posted faraway...

1989-1990

看海

看过了冬天的海，血管中流的一定不再是血
所以做爱时一定要望着大海
一定地你们还在等待
等待海风再次朝向你们
那风一定从床上来

那记亿也是，一定是
死鱼眼中存留的大海的假象
渔夫一定是休假的工程师和牙医
六月地里的棉花一定是药棉
一定地你们还在田间寻找烦恼
你们经过的树木一定被撞出了大包
巨大的怨气一定使你们有与众不同的未来
因为你们太爱说一定
像印度女人一定要露出她们腰里的肉

距离你们合住的地方一定不远
距离唐人街也一定不远
一定会有一个月亮亮得像一口痰
一定会有人说那就是你们的健康
再不重要地或更加重要地，一定地
一定地它留在你们心里
就像英格兰脸上那块傲慢的炮弹皮

WATCHING THE SEA

Having watched the winter sea, what flows in the veins is surely blood
    no more
So when making love one should surely gaze on the ocean
Surely you are still waiting
Waiting for the sea breeze to blow on you once more
That breeze will surely arise from the bed

That remembrance is also, surely is
False images of the ocean preserved in the eyes of dead fish
Fishermen are surely engineers and doctors on vacation
June cotton in the earth is surely cotton swabs
Surely you're all still in the fields seeking vexation
Trees you brush by are surely bruised and swollen
Huge rage surely makes you have a future different from the crowd
Because you are too fond of saying surely
As Indian women will surely reveal their flesh at the waist

The distance to the place you live together is surely not far
The distance to Chinatown is likewise surely not far
Surely there will be a moon shining like a mouthful of spit
Surely there will be people who say that is your health
No longer important, or even more important, surely
Surely it stays in your mind
Just like that arrogant bomb-casing on England's face

看海一定耗尽了你们的年华
眼中存留的星群一定变成了煤渣
大海的阴影一定从海底漏向另一个世界
在反正得有人死去的夜里有一个人一定得死
虽然戒指一定不愿长死在肉里
打了激素的马的屁股却一定要激动
所以整理一定就是乱翻
车链掉了车蹬就一定踏得飞快
春天的风一定像肾结石患者系过的绿腰带
出租汽车司机的脸一定像煮过的水果
你们回家时那把旧椅子一定年轻，一定地

Watching the sea surely uses up your lives
Stars preserved in the eyes have surely become cinders
The ocean's shadow surely seeped from the seabed to another world
In a night when somebody anyhow must die someone surely must die
Although the ring surely does not wish to be long dead on the flesh
Shooting hormones into a horse's ass will surely stir it up
So to arrange tidily is then surely to create disorder
When a bicycle chain falls off peddling surely gets faster
The spring wind surely resembles the kidney stone sufferer's fastened
          green belt
The taxi driver's face surely resembles stewed fruit
When you go home that old chair will surely be young, surely

1989-1990

过海

我们过海，而那条该死的河
该往何处流？

我们回头，而我们身后
没有任何后来的生命

没有任何生命
值得一再地复活？

船上的人，全都木然姑立
亲人们，在遥远的水下呼吸

钟声，持续地响着
越是持久，便越是没有信心

对岸的树像性交中的人
代替海星、海贝和海葵

海滩上散落着针头、药棉
和阴毛——我们望到了彼岸？

所以我们回头，像果实回头
而我们身后——一个墓碑

插进了中学的操场
惟有，惟有在海边哭孩子的妇人

懂得这个冬天有多么地漫长：
没有死人，河便不会有它的尽头……

CROSSING THE SEA

We cross the sea, but that river that would be better off dead
Where should it flow?

We turn around, and behind us
There is no life that follows at all

Is there no life at all
Worth repeatedly resurrecting?

People on the boat, all stand wooden
Relatives, breathe under distant waters

The sound of a bell, steadily tolling
The longer it tolls, the more it lacks faith!

Trees on the far shore are like people having sex
Standing in for sea shells, sea stars, and sea flowers

On the beach are scattered needles, cotton swabs
And pubes — Are we gazing at the other side?

So we turn our heads, like fruits turning their heads
And behind us — a tombstone

Stuck into the high school playground
Only, only women weeping over their children beside the sea

Appreciate how very long this winter will be:
With no dead, the river can have no end…

1990

地图

夜半，有人在窗外诱惑你
烟蒂，像蚕一样爬动起来
桌上，一杯水也动荡起来
你拉开抽屉，里面有一场下了四十年的大雪

一个声音，谁的声音，问：天空就是地图？
你认出呐喊者乌黑的嘴唇
你认出他
正是你，是那个旧你
你认出你的头
正从病院窗口被远远地咳出去——

遥远的地平线上，铁匠和钉子一起移动
救火的人挤在一枚邮票上
正把大海狂泼出去
一些游泳者在水中互相泼水
他们的游泳裤是一些面粉袋
上面印着：远离祖国的钉子们

一阵辛辣的气味
你嗅到风暴最初的信息
像云一样，你循着肉钩荡出肉店的后窗
你身后，有一条腿继续搁在肉案上
你认出那正是你的腿
因你跨过了那一步。

MAP

Midnight, there are people beyond the window enticing you
Cigarette butts, like silkworms start clambering
On the table, a glass of water also starts to churn
You pull open a drawer, inside are forty years of snow

A voice, someone's voice, asks: Is it true the sky's a map?
You recognize the pitch-black lips of the one who cries out
You recognize him
In fact it's you, it's that old you
You recognize your head
Just as it's coughed out into the distance from a hospital window

On the far horizon, blacksmith and saboteur move together
Those fighting fires squeeze onto a postage stamp
As they madly splash out the ocean
Swimmers in the water are splashing one another
Their swimming trunks are flour sacks
Printed with the words: Saboteurs far from the motherland

A whiff of a pungent odor
You sniff out the earliest news of the storm
Like a cloud, following the butcher's hooks you float out the
butcher's back window
Behind you, there's a leg still sitting on the butcher's block
You recognize it as your very own leg
Since you passed over that step.

1990

冬日

黄昏最后的光辉温暖着教堂的尖顶
教堂内的炉火，已经熄灭
呵，时日，时日

我寻找我失落的
并把得到的，放走
用完了墓碑上的字

我闲荡在人间
广大的天地，永恒的父母
祈告，从心头升起

沉默，和声音以外的
融进了与冬天的交流：
风，是孤独的骑马人

云朵，是一堆堆大笑的乡下新娘
十二月神奇的心跳
只是一阵阵旧的朗读

WINTER'S DAY

The very last ray of the setting sun warms the spire
The stove fire in the church, already died out
So, so long ago

I seek what I lost
And what I get, let go
Done with words from a tombstone

I saunter amidst people
Vast world, everlasting parents
Prayers, rise from the heart

Silence, and beyond sound
Melt into winter's exchange:
Wind, is a lonesome rider

Clouds, are huddled laughing country brides
December's mystical palpitations   .
Just bursts of an old recital

1990

我读着

十一月的麦地里我读着我父亲
我读着他的头发
他领带的颜色，他的裤线
还有他的蹄子，被鞋带绊着
阴囊紧缩，颈子因过度的理解伸向天空
我读到我父亲是一匹眼睛大大的马

我读到我父亲曾经短暂地离开过马群
一棵小树上挂着他的外衣
还有他的袜子，还有隐现的马群中
那些苍白的屁股，像剥去肉的
牡蛎壳内盛放的女人洗身的肥皂
我读到我父亲头油的气味
他身上的烟草味
还有他的结核，照亮了一匹马的左肺
我读到一个男孩子的疑问
从一片金色的玉米地里升起
我读到在我懂事的年龄
晾晒谷粒的红房屋顶开始下雨
种麦季节的犁下拖着四条死马的腿
马皮像撑开的伞，还有散于四处的马牙
我读到一张张被时间带走的脸
我读到我父亲的历史在地下静静腐烂
我父亲身上的蝗虫，正独自存在下去

I'M READING

In the November wheat field I'm reading my father
I'm reading his hair
The color of his tie, the crease of his trousers
And his hooves, tripped up by shoelaces
Now skating on ice, now playing the violin
The scrotum shrinks, the neck, knowing too well, stretches toward the sky
I read as far as my father's being a large eyed horse

I read as far as his having temporarily left the herd
His coat hanging from a small tree
And his socks, and appearing indistinctly in the herd
Those pallid buttocks, like a meat-stripped
Oyster shell containing a woman's toilet soap
I read as far as the scent of my father's hair oil
The smell of tobacco on his body
And his tuberculosis, illuminating the left lung of a horse
I read as far as a boy's doubts
Rising out of a patch of golden corn
I read as far as when I was old enough to understand
The red house roofs where grain is dried start to rain
The wheat sowing season's plough drags four dead horse legs
Horse skin like an opened umbrella, and horse teeth scattered everywhere
I read as far as one face after another is carried off by time
I read as far as my father's history silently rotting in the ground
Locusts on my father's body, just continuing to exist alone

像一个白发理发师搂抱着一株衰老的柿子树
我读到我父亲把我重新放回到一匹马腹中去
当我就要变成伦敦雾中的一条石凳
当我的目光越过在银行大道散步的男人……

Like a white-haired barber embracing an aging persimmon tree
I read as far as my father's returning me again to a horse's belly
When I just want to turn into a stone bench in the London fog
When my glance passes over the men strolling down the bank-lined street…

1991

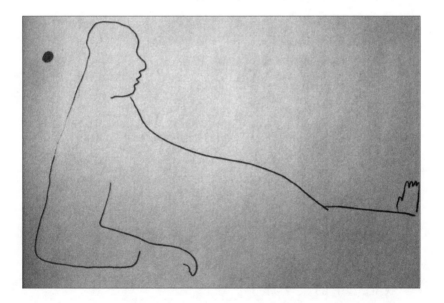

我始终欣喜有一道光在黑夜里

我始终欣喜有一道光在黑夜里
在风声与钟声中我等待那道光
在直到中午才醒来的那个早晨
最后的树叶作梦般地悬着
大量的树叶进入了冬天
落叶从四面把树围拢
树，从倾斜的城市边缘集中了四季的风——

谁让风一直被误解为迷失的中心
谁让我坚持倾听树重新挡住风的声音
为迫使风再度成为收获时节被迫张开的五指
风的阴影从死人手上长出了新叶
指甲被拔出来了，被手。被手中的工具
攥紧，一种酷似人而又被人所唾弃的
像人的阴影，被人走过
是它，驱散了死人脸上最后那道光
却把砍进树林的光，磨得越来越亮

逆着春天的光我走进天亮之前的光里
我认出了那恨我并记住我的惟一的一棵树
在树下，在那棵苹果树下
我记忆中的桌子绿了
骨头被翅膀惊醒的五月的光华，向我展开了
我回头，背上长满青草
我醒着，而天空已经移动

I'VE ALWAYS DELIGHTED IN A SHAFT OF LIGHT
IN THE DEPTH OF NIGHT

I've always delighted in a shaft of light in the depth of night
Midst the sound of wind and bells I await that light
In that morning asleep until noon
The last leaf hangs as if dreaming
Many leaves have entered winter
Leaves falling from all sides hem in the trees
Trees, from the rim of the sloping town gather winds of four seasons ——

Why is the wind always misread as the center of being lost
Why do I intently listen to trees hinder the wind once more
Force the wind to be the harvest season's five prized-open fingers
The wind's shadow grows new leaves from the hands of the dead
Fingernails pulled out, by hand. By tools in hands
Clenched, the spitting image of a human, yet spat on by humans,
Like the shadow of a human, walked over by humans
There it is, driving the last glint of light from the face of the dead
Yet honing ever brighter, the light that slices into the forest!

Against the light of spring I enter the light of before dawn
I recognize the only tree that hates me and has remembered me
Under the tree, under that apple tree
The table in my memory turns green
The splendors of May, bones by wings startled awake, unfold towards me
I turn around, fresh grass has grown over my back
I'm awake, and the sky has already moved

写在脸上的死亡进入了字
被习惯于死亡的星辰所照耀
死亡，射进了光
使孤独的教堂成为测量星光的最后一根柱子
使漏掉的，被剩下。

Death inscribed on the face has entered words
Illuminated by stars accustomed to death
Death, projects into light
Making the solitary church the last pole to measure starlight
Making the left out, left over.

1991

早晨

是早晨或是任何时间，是早晨
你梦到你醒了，你害怕你醒来
所以你说：你害怕绳子，害怕脸
像鸟儿的女人，所以你梦到你父亲
说鸟儿语，喝鸟儿奶
你梦到你父亲是个独身者
在偶然中而不是在梦中
有了你，你梦到你父亲作过的梦
你梦到你父亲说：这是死人作过的梦

你不相信但你倾向于相信
这是梦，仅仅是梦，是你的梦：
曾经是某种自行车的把手
保持着被手攥过的形状
现在，就耷拉在你父亲的小肚子上
曾经是一个拒绝出生的胎儿
现在就是你，正爬回那把手
你梦到了你梦中的一切细节
像你父亲留在地上的牙，闪着光
笑你，所以你并不是死亡
只是其中一例：你梦到了你梦的死亡。

MORNING

Whether morning or whenever, it's morning
You dream of your waking, you're frightened of waking
So you say: You're frightened of rope, frightened of faces
Looking like bird women, so you dream of your father
Speak bird talk, drink bird milk
You dream that your father is a celibate
By chance, and not in dream
He had you, you dream of your father's dreamed dreams
You dream your father says: This is a dream dreamed by the dead.

You don't believe it but you incline to believing
This is dream, merely dream, your dream:
It was the handlebar of a certain bicycle
Retaining the shape of the hand's grip
Now, drooping down on your father's little belly
Once a fetus which refused to be born
It's now you, climbing back to the handlebar
You've dreamed of all the details in your dream
Like your father's teeth lying on the ground, sparkling
Laughing at you, so you certainly are not death itself
Merely an example: you've dreamed of your dream's death.

1991

没有

没有人向我告别
没有人彼此告别
没有人向死人告别，这早晨开始时

没有它自身的边际

除了语言，朝向土地被失去的边际
除了郁金香盛开的鲜肉，朝向深夜不闭的窗户
除了我的窗户，朝向我不再懂得的语言

没有语言

只有光反复折磨着，折磨着
那只反复拉动在黎明的锯
只有郁金香骚动着，直至不再骚动

没有郁金香

只有光，停滞在黎明
星光，播洒在疾驰列车沉睡的行李间内
最后的光，从婴儿脸上流下

没有光

THERE IS NO

There is no one bidding me farewell
There is no one bidding another farewell
There is no one bidding the dead farewell, when this morning starts

There is no border to itself

Except for language, facing land's lost borders
Except for tulips' flourishing fresh flesh, facing windows unclosed
        unto the night
Except for my window, facing my no longer comprehensible language

There is no language

Only light repeatedly grinding, grinding
That repeatedly worked saw at daybreak
Only that restive tulip, until restive no more

There are no tulips

Only light, stuck at dawn
Star light, sprinkling into the express train's slumbering baggage car
The last light, trickles off a baby's face

There is no light

我用斧劈开肉，听到牧人在黎明的尖叫
我打开窗户，听到光与冰的对喊
是喊声让雾的锁链崩裂

没有喊声

只有土地
只有土地和运谷子的人知道
只在午夜鸣叫的鸟是看到过黎明的鸟

没有黎明

I use an axe to split open meat, hear the sharp cry of the shepherd at dawn
I open the window, hear the yelling between light and ice
It's the yelling makes fog's fetters crack open

There is no yelling

Only land
Only land and he who transports grain who know
Only the bird which calls at midnight is the bird who has seen dawn

There is no dawn

1991

他们

手指插在裤袋里玩着零钱和生殖器
他们在玩成长的另一种方法

在脱衣舞女撅起的臀部间
有一个小小的教堂，用三条白马的腿走动起来了

他们用鼻子把它看见
而他们的指甲将在五月的地里发芽

五月的黄土地是一堆堆平坦的炸药
死亡模拟它们，死亡的理由也是

在发情的铁器对土壤最后的刺激中
他们将成为被牺牲的田野的一部分

死人死前死去已久的寂静
使他们懂得的一切都不再改变

他们固执地这样想，他们做
他们捐出了童年

使死亡保持完整
他们套用了我们的经历。

THEY

Fingers stuck into pants pockets jingling coins and genitals
They're playing at another way of growing up

Between the striptease artist's elevated buttocks
There is a tiny church, starting to walk on three white horse legs

They use noses to see it
But their fingernails will sprout in the May soil

The yellow earth of May is mound upon mound of flat explosives
Imitated by death, and the reason for death is also

In the very last jolt to the soil of the ironware in heat
They will become a part of the sacrificed wilderness

The silence of the long dead dead before dying
Made all they understood change no more

Their stubborn way of thinking, their doing
Their giving away childhood

Kept death intact
They made reckless use of our experience.

1991

抓马蜂的男孩

没有风的时候，有鸟
"有鸟，但是没有早晨"

抓马蜂的男孩从一幅画的右侧进入
树的叫声，被鸟接过去了

"小妈妈，你拥有的麦田向着我"
三个太阳追着一只鸟

"小妈妈，你肚子里的小牛动起来啦"
世上最黑的一匹马驰来

"小妈妈，棺材是从南方运来的"
树木量着，量着孩子的头

孩子的呼喊，被留在一只梨里
更多的人，被留在画面之外

孩子曾用五只脚站立
他现在的脚是沙

长不出叶子的幼树开始哭泣
一只熟透的李子接着叫 "你们—我们"

THE BOY WHO CATCHES WASPS

When there is no wind, there are birds
"There are birds, but there is no morning"

The boy who catches wasps enters from the left side of a painting
The call of the trees, has been intercepted by birds

"Little Mama, wheat fields you possess favor me"
Three suns chasing one bird

"Little Mama, the calf in your belly has moved"
The blackest horse in the world gallops up

"Little Mama, the coffin comes from the south"
The trees are weighing, weighing the child's head

The child's screams, have been left inside a pear
Even more people, have been left outside the painting

The child uses five legs to stand
Now his legs are sand

Saplings unable to sprout leaves start to weep
A ripened plum then cries out "You — Us"

1992

在墓地

在墓地，而没有回忆
有叹息，但是被推迟
蒙着脸，跪下去

唱

没人要我们，我们在一起
是我们背后的云，要我们靠在一起
我们背后的树，彼此靠得更近

唱

因为受辱
雪从天上来，因为祝福
风在此地，此地便是遗忘
越是远离麦地，便越是孤独

收听

然后收割，寒冷，才播种
忍受，所以经久
相信，于是读出：

有

有一个飞翔的家——在找我们。

IN THE GRAVEYARD

In the graveyard, and there are no recollections
There are sighs, but they are deferred
Faces covered, kneeling down

Singing

No one wants us, we are together
It's the clouds behind us, want us to huddle together
The trees behind us, huddle even closer

Singing

Since humiliated
Snow comes from the sky, since fortunate
The wind is here, so here is forgetting
The further from the wheat field, the lonelier

Listening in

Then gathering in, icy cold, then sowing
Enduring, therefore durable
Believing, thereupon read out:

There is

There is a home with wings —— seeking us out.

1992

在这样一种天气里

来自天气的任何意义都没有

土地没有幅员，铁轨朝向没有方向
被一场做完的梦所拒绝
被装进一只鞋匣里
被一种无法控诉所控制
在虫子走过的时间里
畏惧死亡的人更加依赖畏惧

        在这样一种天气里
        你是那天气的一个间隙

你望着什么，你便被它所忘却
吸着它呼出来的，它便钻入你的气味
望到天亮之前的变化
你便找到变为草的机会
从人种下的树木经过
你便遗忘一切

        在这样一种天气里
        你不会站在天气一边

IN WEATHER SUCH AS THIS
NO MEANING AT ALL
IS TO BE HAD FROM WEATHER

Land has no boundary, railroad tracks no direction
Rejected by a dreamed-out dream
Stuffed into a shoebox
Controlled by a sort of lack of means of denouncing
In the time an insect takes to walk by
Those fearful of death increase their dependence on fear

> In weather such as this
> You are an interval in the weather

Whatever you stare at you are forgotten by
Inhaling what it exhales, it bores into your smell
Staring upon the change before daybreak
You find the opportunity to turn into grass
Passing by trees grown by people
You forget everything

> In weather such as this
> You won't stand by weather's side

也不会站在信心那边，只会站在虚构一边
当马蹄声不再虚构词典
请你的舌头不要再虚构马蜂
当麦子在虚构中成熟，然后烂掉
请吃掉夜驾歌声中最后的那只李子吧
吃掉，然后把冬天的音响留到枝上

在这样一种天气里
只有虚构在进行

Nor will you stand by faith, only by the side of fabrication
When horses' hooves no longer fabricate dictionaries
Ask your tongue to fabricate hornets no more
When wheat in fabrication matures, afterwards rots away
Would you please eat up that last plum in the nightingale's song
Eat it up, then leave the sound of winter on the branch

        In weather such as this
        Only fabrication advances

1992

一刻

街头大提琴师鸣响回忆的一刻
黄昏天空的最后一块光斑，在死去
死在一个旧火车姑上

一只灰色的内脏在天空敞开了
没有什么在它之外了
除了一个重量，继续坐在河面上
那曾让教堂眩晕的重量
现在，好象只是寂静

大提琴声之后只有寂静
树木静静改变颜色
孩子们静静把牛奶喝下去
运沙子的船静静驶过
我们望着，像瓦静静望着屋顶
我们嗅着，谁和我们在一起时的空气
已经静静死去

谁存在着，只是光不再显示
谁离开了自己，只有一刻
谁說那一刻就是我们的一生
而此刻，苏格兰的雨声
突然敲响了一只盆一

INSTANT

The instant the sound of the street cellist recollects
In the sky at dusk the last brilliant fleck of sunlight, is dying out
Dying over an old railroad station

A gray intestine opens wide in the sky
Outside it there is nothing
Except for a weight, still sitting atop the river's surface
That was the weight of the church shimmering
Now, it seems there is only silence

After the sound of the cello there is only silence
Trees quietly change color
Children quietly drink their milk
The sand freighter quietly sails by
We watch, like tiles quietly watching a roof
We sniff, the air of when whoever and we were together
It's already quietly died out

Whoever existed, is was only light displayed no more
Whoever left themselves, it was only an instant
Whoever said that instant was our whole life
And this instant, the sound of Scottish rain
Suddenly pattering on a basin —

1992

静默

在等待暴风雪的窗口悬挂你的肖像
在一只黑盘子中盛放面包
手，伸向没有手存在的地方

　　　是静默

雪，在这时降下
你，正被马注视着
那复雪的坡，是一些念头

　　　是你的静默

墓园中，默默移动着羊群
鸦群密布的天空，已经破晓
一个得到允许的静默
在墓石上纪录：

　　　沉思，是静默的中断

窗外的世界静默不语
在白色的风景中静默不语
钟表嘀嗒，指针不动
手下，纸上，有这样一个处境：

　　　寻找人以外的。

SILENT TRIBUTE

The window waiting for the snowstorm hangs up your portrait
Offering bread in a black dish
Hands, stretching towards a place where hands do not exist

      Is silent tribute

Snow, at this very moment falls
You, are right now being stared at by a horse
That twice snowed upon slope, is thoughts

      Is silent tribute

In the graveyard, a silently moving flock of sheep
The sky thick with a flock of crows, is already dawning
A silent tribute which has got permission
On a tombstone is recorded:

      Meditation, is the rupture of silent tribute

Silent tribute in the world outside the window is quiet
Silent tribute in the white-colored landscape is quiet
Clocks tick, the compass needle is still
Under the hand, on the paper, is a plight like this:

      Seeking something beyond humanity.

1992

常 常

常常她们占据公园的一把铁椅
一如她们常常拥有许多衣服
她们拥有的房子里也曾有过人生
这城市常常被她们梦着
这世界也是

一如她们度过的漫长岁月
常常她们在读报时依旧感到饥饿
那来自遥远国度的饥饿
让她们觉得可以胖了，只是一种痛苦
虽然她们的生活不会因此而改变
她们读报时，地图确实变大了

她们做过情人、妻子、母亲，到现在还是
只是没人愿意记得她们
连她们跟谁一块儿睡过的枕头
也不再记得。所以
她们跟自己谈话的时间越来越长
好像就是对着主。所以
她们现在是善良的，如果原来不是

她们愿意倾听了，无论对人
对动物，或对河流，常常
她们觉得自己就是等待船只

OFTEN

Often they occupy a metal chair in the park
Just as they often own many clothes
In the houses they own lives have also been lived
This town is often dreamt of by them
This world is also

Just as in the long slow years they have spent
Often while reading the newspaper they feel hungry like before
That hunger that comes from a far country
Makes them feel they can get fat, it's just a sort of suffering
Although their lives cannot change because of this
When they read the newspaper, the map gets truly bigger

They have been lovers, wives, mothers, and still are
But no one wants to remember them
Even the pillow they slept on with another
Does not remember. So
They spend longer and longer chatting to themselves
It's just as if they were facing God. So
They are good now, if at first they were not

They want to listen closely now, whether to people
To animals, or to rivers, often
They feel themselves to be the same port
Waiting for boats to leave or arrive
They do not necessarily want to go to Africa

离去或到来的同一个港口
她们不一定要到非洲去
只要坐在那把固定的铁椅上
她们对面的流亡者就能盖着苹果树叶
睡去，睡去并且梦着
梦到她们的子宫是一座明天的教堂。

But rather to sit on that regular metal chair
The exile opposite them can only cover up with apple tree leaves
And sleep, sleep and dream
It's as if their wombs were tomorrow's church.

1992

在一起

灯亮着
我们在一起
在没有灯光的一半里
我们的记忆
在它以外
在光无力到达的一半里
我们想象它
由于没有想象力
我们抽着烟
也许是过早地
我们在一起
灯更亮
是灯，不是光
我们在一起
因为我们怕
因为母亲飞着
在一只炉子里
像一只蛾子
我们怕
我们搂得更紧
在等待母亲燃烧
燃尽的时间里
我们没有睫毛
从不睡觉

TOGETHER

The lamp is lit
We are together
In that part where is no light
Our memory
Beyond it
In that part that the light cannot reach
We imagine it
For lack of imagination
We smoke a cigarette
Perhaps it's too early
We are together
The lamp shines brighter
It's the lamp, not the light
We are together
Because we are afraid
Because mother is flying
In a stove
Like a moth
We are afraid
We huddle closer
While waiting for mother to burn
In the time it takes to burn out
We have no eyelashes
From not sleeping
There is no way to describe ourselves
That's not possible

无法形容自己
那不可能
尤如不能选择
我们是婴儿
但不是具体的

我们是婴儿脑子中浮动的冰山.

Just as if we couldn't choose
We are babes
But not real babes

We are icebergs floating in the brains of babes.

1992

什么时候我知道铃声是绿色的

从树的任何方向我都接受天空
树间隐藏着橄榄绿的字
像光隐藏在词典里

被逝去的星辰记录着
被瞎了眼的鸟群平衡着，光
和它的阴影，死和将死

两只梨荡着，在树上
果实有最初的阴影
像树间隐藏的铃声

在树上，十二月的风抵抗着更烈的酒
有一阵风，催促话语的来临
被谷仓的立柱挡着，挡住

被大理石的恶梦梦着，梦到
被风走下墓碑的声响惊动，惊醒
最后的树叶向天空奔去

秋天的书写，从树的死亡中萌发
铃声，就在那时照亮我的脸
在最后一次运送黄金的天空——

THE TIME I KNEW THE BELL-SOUND WAS GREEN

From whichever way the tree faces I accept the sky
In the trees hide olive green words
Like light hiding in a dictionary

Recorded by stars that have passed on
Balanced by flocks of blinded birds, light
And its shadow, death and death to come

Two pears swaying, on the tree
Fruit has the earliest shadow
Like the bell-sound hiding in the trees

On the trees, December wind resists yet fiercer wine
There is a gust of wind, hastening the arrival of discourse
Blocked by the upright post of the granary, blocked off

Dreamt by the marble stone's bad dream, dreaming of
Being startled by the sound of the wind going down
          to the tombstone, startled awake
The last leaf flees to the sky

Autumn's writing, bursts from the tree's death
Just then, the bell-sound, illuminates my face
For the last time delivering a golden sky —

1992

为了

拖着一双红鞋趟过满地的啤酒盖
为了双腿间有一个永恒的敌意
肿胀的腿伸入水中搅动
为了骨头在肉里受气
为了脚趾间游动的小鱼
为了有一种教育
从黑皮肤中流走了柏油
为了土地，在这双脚下受了伤
为了它，要永无止境地铸造里程

用失去指头的手指着
为了众民族赤身裸体地迁移
为了没有死亡的地点，也不会再有季节
为了有哭声，而这哭声并没有价格
为了所有的，而不是仅有的
为了那永不磨灭的
已被歪曲，为了那个歪曲
已扩张为一张完整的地图
从，从血污中取出每日的图画吧—

BECAUSE

Holding a pair of red shoes wading through beer tops littering the ground
Because in between the pair of legs there is an eternal animosity
Swollen legs stretching in to shake up the water
Because bones in meat are bullied
Because of little fish swimming in between toes
Because of having an education
Pitch flows out of black skin
Because of the earth, wounded under this pair of feet
Because of it, endlessly cast milestones.

Pointing with hands that have lost their fingers
Because of nations migrating nakedly
Because of places that have not died, and will never again have seasons
Because there is crying, and this crying has no price at all
Because wholly, and not simply
Because of that unerasable
Distortion, because of that distortion
Extended into an entire map
And what if we take each day's picture out, out of the bloodstain —

1993

那些岛屿

是一些真正离开鞋的脚趾
它们在逃避中形成，而它们留驻了土地
它们是脑子中存留的真正的瘤子
而它们留驻了时间
在不动的风景中经历变迁
在海浪的每一次冲击中说：不
它们的孤独来自海底
来自被鱼吃剩的水手的脸
来自留恋惊涛骇浪的人

没有牙齿人的喊声曾经到达那里
孤独，曾在那里被判为拯救
当我随同旅游者，像假珠子一样
泻到它们的码头上，我
望到我投向海底的影子
一张挂满珍珠的犁
犁开了存留于脑子中的墓地：
在那里，在海军基地大笑的沙子底下
尚有，尚有供词生长的有益的荒地。

THOSE ISLANDS

Are really toes which have discarded shoes
They take shape in flight, yet they retain the soil
They are real tumors that remain in the brain
Retaining time
In motionless landscape experience shifts
In the crashing of every wave say: no
Their loneliness comes from the seabed
Comes from the remains of sailors' faces left over by fish
Comes from those who crave stormy seas

The cries of the toothless have reached there
The lonely, have there been judged the saviors
When I follow travelers, it's like false pearls
Flowing swiftly to their jetty, I
Stare at the shadow I cast to the seabed
A plow hung all over with pearls
Plowing up the burial ground which has remained in the brain:
Over there, midst the laughing sand of the naval base
There still is, still is a beneficial wasteland providing
        for the growth of words.

1993

五年

五杯烈酒，五枝腊烛，五年
四十三岁，一阵午夜的大汗
五十个巴掌扇向桌面
一群攥紧双拳的鸟儿从昨天飞来

五挂红鞭放响五月，五指间雷声隆隆
而四月四匹死马舌头上寄生的四朵毒蘑菇不死
五日五时五分五枝腊烛熄灭
而黎明时分大叫的风景不死
头发死而舌头不死
从煮熟的肉中找回的脾气不死
五十年水银渗透精液而精液不死
胎儿自我接生不死
五年过去，五年不死
五年内，二十代虫子死光。

FIVE YEARS

Five glasses of strong liquor, five candles, five years
Forty-three years, an outbreak of sweat at midnight
Fifty hands flap towards the table top
A flock of birds clenching their fists fly in from yesterday

Five strings of red crackers applaud the fifth month, thunder
        rumbles between five fingers
And four parasitic poisonous mushrooms on four dead horses'
        tongues in the fourth month do not die
Five days five hours five minutes five candles are extinguished
Yet the landscape summoned at dawn does not die
Hair dies but tongues do not die
The spirit discovered in the cooked meat does not die
Fifty years of mercury seeps into semen and semen does not die
The fetus's self-delivery does not die
Five years pass, five years do not die
Within five years, twenty generations of insects die out.

1994

依旧是

走在额头飘雪的夜里而依旧是
从一张白纸上走过而依旧是
走进那看不见的田野而依旧是

走在词间，麦田间，走在
减价的皮鞋间，走到词
望到家乡的时刻，而依旧是

站在麦田间整理西装，而依旧是
屈下黄金盾牌铸造的膝盖，而依旧是
这世上最响亮的，最响亮的

　　依旧是，依旧是大地

一道秋光从割草人腿间穿过时，它是
一片金黄的玉米地里有一阵狂笑声，是它
一阵鞭炮声透出鲜红的辣椒地，它依旧是

任何排列也不能再现它的金黄
它的秩序是秋日原野的一阵奋力生长
它有无处不在的说服力，它依旧是它

一阵九月的冷牛粪被铲向空中而依旧是
十月的石头走成了队伍而依旧是
十一月的雨经过一个没有了你的地点而依旧是

JUST LIKE IT USED TO BE

Walking in a night when snow flutters on the forehead
      just like it used to be
Walking over from a blank page just like it used to be
Walking into that invisible field just like it used to be

Walking among words, among wheat fields, walking
Among discounted shoes, walking up to words
Seeing home, that moment, just like it used to be

Straightening western clothes in the wheat field,
      just like it used to be
Kneeling on kneecaps cast from a gold shield,
      just like it used to be
This world's most resounding, most resounding

      just like it used to be, is the Earth just like it used to be

A time when a ray of autumn light shone between
      the grass mower's legs, it is
A burst of wild laughter within a stretch of golden corn, is it
A burst of firecrackers spurting out of the scarlet chili patch,
      just like they used to

No arrangement whatsoever can reproduce its gilt
Its order is a burst of furious growth in the prairie
      on an autumn day
It has ubiquitous powers of persuasion, it is just like it used to

依旧是七十只梨子在树上笑歪了脸
你父亲依旧是你母亲
笑声中的一阵咳嗽声

牛头向着逝去的道路颠簸
而依旧是一家人坐在牛车上看雪
被一根巨大的牛舌舔到

　　温暖啊，依旧是温暖

是来自记忆的雪，增加了记忆的重量
是雪欠下的，这时雪来覆盖
是雪翻过了那一页

　　翻过了，而依旧是

冬日的麦地和墓地已经接在一起
四棵凄凉的树就种在这里
昔日的光涌进了诉说，在话语以外崩裂

　　崩裂，而依旧是

A pat of cold September cow dung shoveled into the air
     just like it used to be
October's stones serried into ranks just like they used to be
November rain passes through a place where you are not
     just like it used to

Just like they used to seventy pears on the tree smile a crooked smile
Your father is your mother just like he used to be
A fit of coughing in the midst of laughter

The ox's head jolts along the extinguished road
And just like they used to a whole family rides the ox cart watching
     the snow
Licked by an enormous ox tongue

     So warm, warm like it used to be

It's snow comes from memory, increasing the weight of memory
It's absence of snow, at this time not yet covered by snow
It's that page snow turned over

     Turned over, just like it used to be

Winter's wheat fields and burial grounds have already joined up
Four desolate trees grow right here
Light of former days gushes into the narration, fragments
     beyond discourse

     Fragments, just like it used to

你父亲用你母亲的死做他的天空
用他的死做你母亲的墓碑
你父亲的骨头从高高的山冈上走下

　　而依旧是

每一粒星星都在经历此生此世
埋在后园的每一块碎玻璃都在说话
为了一个不会再见的理由，说

　　依旧是，依旧是

Your father turns your mother's death into his sky
Turns his death into your mother's tombstone
Your father's bones walk down from the high hill

    Just like they used to

Each star is experiencing this life and world
Each shaft of broken glass buried in the backyard is talking
For a motive that will not be seen again, says

    Like it used to be, like it used to be

1993

它们

——纪念西尔维亚·普拉斯

裸露，是它们的阴影
像鸟的呼吸

它们在这个世界之外
在海底;像牡蛎

吐露，然后自行闭合
留下孤独

可以孕育出珍珠的孤独
留在它们的阴影之内

在那里，回忆是冰山
是鲨鱼头做的纪念馆

是航行，让大海变为灰色
像伦敦，一把撑开的黑伞

在你的死亡里存留着
是雪花，盲文，一些数字

但不会是回忆
让孤独，转变为召唤

THEM

In memory of Sylvia Plath

Exposure, is their shadow
Like a bird's breathing

They are beyond this world
On the seabed, like oysters

Revealing themselves, then closing up
Leaving behind solitude

A solitude that can give birth to pearls
Remains within their shadow

There, recollections are icebergs
Are a memorial hall made from a shark's head

Are navigation, making the ocean turn gray
Like London, an open black umbrella

Preserved in your death
Are snowflakes, braille, some numbers

But it cannot be recollections
Making solitude, turn into a summons

让最孤独的彻夜搬动桌椅
让他们用吸尘器

把你留在人间的气味
全部吸光，已满三十年了。

Making the loneliest move tables and chairs all night long
Making them use vacuum cleaners

To suck away all the fragrance of your stay in this world,
For all of thirty years now.

1993

从不作梦

隔着人世做饼，用
烤面包上孩子留下的齿痕
做床，接过另一只奶嘴
作只管飞翔的鸟
不哭，不买保险
不是祈祷出来的
不在这秩序里

　　从不作梦

作无风的夜里熄灭的腊烛
作星光，照耀骑马人的后颈
作只生一季的草，作诗
作冻在树上的犁
作黑麦，在风中忍受沉思

　　从不作梦

作风，大声吆喝土地
作一滴水，无声滴下
作马背上掠过的痉挛
作可能孵化出父亲的卵
从夺来的时间里
失眠的时间里，纪念星辰
在头顶聚敛谜语的好时光！

NEVER BEING A DREAMER

Being a cake alongside the human world, using
Tooth marks left by children in a piece of toast
As a bed, pulling over the other nipple
Being a bird that only likes to circle
Not weeping, not buying insurance
It's not the product of prayer
It's not in this order

    Never being a dreamer

Being an extinguished candle in a breezeless night
Being starlight, shining on the nape of the horse rider's neck
Being grass that sprouts but for one season, being a poet
Being a pear frozen on a tree
Being black wheat, enduring deep thought in the wind

    Never being a dreamer

Being wind, yelling loudly at the earth
Being a water drop, silently dripping
Being the convulsion rippling along the horse's back
Being the one able to hatch out the father's egg
From eerie time
From sleepless time, commemorating stars
In that moment good for the invention of riddles!

1994

锁住的方向

是失业的锁匠们最先把你望到
当你飞翔的臀部穿过苹果树影
一个厨师阴沉的脸，转向田野

当舌头们跪着，渐渐跪成同一个方向
它们找不到能把你说出来的那张嘴
它们想说，但说不出口

　　　说：还有两粒橄榄

在和你接吻时，能变得坚实
还有一根舌头，能够作打开葡萄酒瓶的螺旋锥
还有两朵明天的云，拥抱在河岸
有你和谁接过的吻，正在变为遍地生长的野草莓

　　　舌头同意了算什么

是玉米中有谜语！历史朽烂了
而大理石咬你的脖子
两粒橄榄，谜语中的谜语
支配鸟头内的磁石，动摇古老的风景
让人的虚无在两根水泥柱子间徘徊去吧

　　　死人才有灵魂

LOCKED DIRECTION

It was the unemployed locksmiths who were the very first to direct your gaze
When your hovering buttocks passed through the shadow of the apple tree
To the glum face of a cook, turning towards the fields

When tongues kneel down, gradually kneel in the same direction
They cannot find the mouth that can say you
They want to say something, but cannot manage to

Say: There are still two olives

When kissing you, can become robust
And there is another tongue, which can be a wine bottle corkscrew
And there are two clouds on a clear day, embracing on the river bank
There's the kiss you shared with another, right now becoming the
wild strawberries that grow in the borderlands

What's it matter that tongues are agreed

It's in the midst of corn that there are riddles! History's decayed
And marble bites your neck
Two olives, riddles within riddles
Control the magnet in the bird's head, shaking ancient scenery
Maybe making people's nothingness vacillate between two pillars of cement

Only then will the dead have souls

在一条撑满黑伞的街上
有一袋沉甸甸的桔子就要被举起来了
从一只毒死的牡蛎内就要敞开另一个天空
马头内，一只大理石浴盆破裂：

绿色的时间就要降临

一只冻在冰箱里的鸡渴望着
两粒赖在烤羊腿上的葡萄干渴望着
从一个无法预报的天气中

从诱惑男孩子尿尿的滴水声中
从脱了脂的牛奶中
从最后一次手术中
渴望，与金色的沙子一道再次闯入风暴

从熏肉的汗腺和暴力的腋窝中升起的风暴

当浮冰，用孕妇的姿态继续漂流
渴望，是他们惟一留下的词
当你飞翔的臀部打开了锁不住的方向
用赤裸的肉体阻挡长夜的流逝
他们留下的词，是穿透水泥的精子——

On a street of black umbrellas
There's a heavy bag of oranges about to be picked up
From within a poisonous oyster another sky is about to open up
In the horse's head, a marble bathtub cracks:

Green time approaches

A frozen chicken in the refrigerator earnestly hopes
Two raisins dependent on the roast leg of lamb earnestly hope
From within unforcastable weather
From within the dripping sound of coaxing a boy to pee
From within the skimmed milk
From within the last operation
Earnestly hope, together with golden sand to blaze once again into the storm

A storm rises from within the sweat glands of smoked meat
and the armpits of violence

When ice floes, deploy the posture of pregnant women to stay afloat
Earnestly hope, are the only words they leave behind
When your hovering buttocks break open locked direction
Obstruct with naked flesh the passing of the long night
The words they leave, are the sperm that pierce through cement —

1994

锁不住的方向

是失业的锁匠们最后把你望到
当你飞翔的臀部穿过烤栗子人的昏迷
一个厨师捂住脸，跪向田野

当舌头们跪着，渐渐跪向不同的方向
它们找到了能把你说出来的嘴
却不再说。说，它们把它废除了

据说：还有两粒橄榄

在和你接吻时，可以变得坚实
据说有一根舌头，可以代替打开葡萄酒瓶的螺旋锥
谁说有两朵明天的云，曾拥抱在河岸
是谁和谁接过的吻，己变为遍地生长的野草莓

玉米同意了不算什么

是影子中有玉米。历史朽烂了
有大理石的影子咬你的脖子
两粒橄榄的影子，影子中的影子
拆开鸟头内的磁石，支配鸟嗉囊中的沙粒
让人的虚无停滞于两根水泥柱子间吧

死人也不再有灵魂

UNLOCKABLE DIRECTION

It was the unemployed locksmiths who were the last to direct your gaze
When your hovering buttocks pierced through the roast chestnut man's coma
To a cook's covered up face, kneeling towards the fields

When tongues kneel down, gradually kneel in different directions
They find the mouth that can say you
But say no more. Say, they abolish it

      Hear say: There are still two olives

When kissing you, may become robust
Hear say there is a tongue, may replace a wine bottle corkscrew
Who says there are two clouds on a clear day, embracing on a river bank
Whose kiss was shared with whom, became the wild strawberries that
      grow in the borderlands

      It doesn't matter that the corn agreed

It's in the midst of shadow that there's corn. History's decayed
There are shadows of marble biting your neck
The shadows of two olives, shadow within shadows
Break open the magnet in the bird's head, controlling the salad in the
      bird's crop
Maybe making people's nothingness stagnate between two pillars of cement

      The dead will never again have souls

在一条曾经撑满黑伞的街上
有一袋沉甸甸的桔子到底被举起来了
灰色的天空，从一只毒死的牡蛎内翻开了一个大剧场
马头内的思想，像电灯丝一样清晰：

　　　　绿色的时间在演出中到临

一只冻在冰箱里的鸡醒来了
两粒赖在烤羊腿上的葡萄干醒来了
从一个已被预报的天气中
从抑制男孩子尿尿的滴水声中
从脱了脂的精液中
从一次无力完成的手术中
醒来，与金色的沙子一道再次闯入风暴

　　　　从淋浴喷头中喷出的风暴

当孕妇，用浮冰的姿态继续漂流
漂流，是他们最后留下的词
当你飞翔的臀部锁住那锁不住的方向
用赤裸的坦白供认长夜的流逝
他们留下的精子，是被水泥砌死的词。

On a street once filled with black umbrellas
There's a heavy bag of oranges that has finally been picked up
Gray skies, from within a poisonous oyster flick open a big stage prop
The thought in the horse's head, as clear as a light bulb filament:

In a performance green time approaches

A frozen chicken in a refrigerator wakes up
Two raisins dependent on a roast leg of lamb wake up
From within already forecast weather
From the dripping sound of inhibiting a boy's peeing
From within skimmed sperm
From within an operation there wasn't strength to complete
Wake up, together with golden sand once again blaze into the storm

A storm that bursts out from within the shower head

When pregnant women, deploy the posture of ice floes to stay afloat
Floating, is the only word they leave behind
When your hovering buttocks lock up that unlockable direction
Confess with naked candor the passing of the long night
The sperm they leave behind, are words built to death by cement.

1994

归来

从甲板上认识大海
瞬间，就认出它巨大的徘徊

从海上认识犁，瞬间
就认出我们有过的勇气

在每一个瞬间，仅来自
每一个独个的恐惧

从额头顶着额头，站在门坎上
说再见，瞬间就是五年

从手攥着手攥得紧紧地，说松开
瞬间，鞋里的沙子已全部来自大海

刚刚，在烛光下学会阅读
瞬间，背囊里的重量就减轻了

刚刚，在咽下粗面包时体会
瞬间，瓶中的水已被放回大海

被来自故乡的牛瞪着，云
叫我流泪，瞬间我就流

RETURNING

Recognizing the ocean from the deck
In an instant, make out its enormous peregrinations

On the sea recognize a plough, in an instant
Making out the courage we had

At each instant, only coming from
Each solitary fear

Forehead against forehead, standing on the threshold
Saying goodbye, in an instant five years have past

Hand tightly grasping hand, saying let go
In an instant, the sand in the shoes has come entirely from the ocean

Just now, by candlelight learnt to read
In an instant, the weight of the backpack lessened

Just now, while swallowing coarse bread felt
In an instant, the water in the bottle had been returned to the ocean

Stared at by an ox from the home country, saying
Make me weep, in an instant I weep

But whichever way I go
In an instant, it turns to drifting

但我朝任何方向走
瞬间，就变成漂流

刷洗被单簧管麻痹的牛背
记忆，瞬间就找到源头

词，瞬间就走回词典
但在词语之内，航行

让从未开始航行的人
永生——都不得归来。

Scrubbing an ox's back benumbed by a clarinet
Remembering, in an instant has found its source

Words, in an instant make their way back to dictionaries
But within words, navigation

Renders those who have not yet begun navigating
Forever — all incapable of returning

1994

节日

1

除了我你没有别的树
你就是我的城市，它原来的样子
保护着我的障碍，你的腿已不必用力夹紧

　　　那就是现在

许多发明绕过了它，它们带走了季节
走向婚姻的虫子，和肥堆。那就是追
所显现的一个类似无限的大坑

　　　现在并不明确

在我的胎盘还未学会咳嗽之前
你的指甲，已经抓着并不存在的墙壁
指环，已经牵动你的指尖去触摸

　　　这样的一个进程

在无人记录的夏天，指头带来的风云
诱出了蜗角，带出了蜗体，腾空了蜗壳
跟上了速度，这样的一种立场。像神的立场

　　　只与部分时间共同向前吧

HOLIDAYS

1

Apart from me you have no other tree
You are my town, the way it was before
Protecting my defenses, your legs no longer need to squeeze so tight

That's the present

Many discoveries bypassed it, they carried off seasons
Towards the matrimonial insects, and heaps of fat. That's pursuing
A revealed seemingly limitless big pit

The present is not clear at all

At a time when my placenta had not yet learned to cough
Your finger nails, were already clutching at walls that did not exist at all
Rings on your fingers, were already influencing your finger tips, to touch

A process such as this

In a summer recorded by no one, the wind and clouds that fingers brought
Lured out snails' horns, brought out snails' bodies, soared up high on snail shells
Gathering speed, a position such as this. Like the position of gods

Perhaps just for a part of the time going forward in concert

2

英语光线支配下的天空，仅在这一点转暗
缓慢的行程，比海边的奇景，蛹的进化
比速度还要固执，那就是它最重要的遗产了
锚，触到海底的声响已被听到，但是掺进了杂音

那就是激情了

是它在又一次问，当下一次已在此次之中
问的声音就更低了。树，也克服了来自内在的风
树影，却继续摇晃着。你的手
搁在我的腿间，也像忘了一样

那就是与翅膀的告别了

树木也在加深颜色，在绿色以外。多久了
你就是光，无论光是什么，你还是你
直到你不再是，你醒了，整座果园还醉
你的眼睛转到下午 5 点钟的太阳
你姥姥桌上的 60 只苹果，还在闪闪发亮

2

A sky allotted by the rays of English language, only at this point turns dark,
Slow travel, compared to the beauty of the seacoast, the evolution of larvae
Even more stable than speed, now that's its most important legacy
The anchor, the sound of its touching the seabed is heard, but the added noise

Now that's passion

It's it questioning once more, when next time is already in this time
The questioning voice is deeper. The tree, has also overcome the wind
      from within
The tree's shadow, however continues to sway. Your hand
Placed between my legs, also seems like it's forgotten

Now that's a farewell to wings

Trees are also deepening their color, beyond green. For so long
You have been light, no matter what light is, you are still you
Until you are no more, you're awake, sitting right in the orchard still drunk
Your eyes turn to the five-in-the-afternoon sun
Sixty apples on your grandmother's table, are still twinkling

凌晨一点，光向郊外散去，我望着你，你
也望着你，在留给你的那场雾里，我倾听
云，倾听天空，也倾听你洗碟子时的流水声

"这文明一定要屹立下去"

一个四肢挂满海马的女人浮现了，随即
像一片药一样化开，过去，被你的身体存留着
它创造了我的记忆：我和你，曾是两块
石头，拥抱在一家大歌剧院的门楣上

那就是等待

当黑夜从白天开始，许多平行的欧洲的大河
也像停在提琴上的弓那样，等待一双手
追上来，像众神只在夜间寻找女人的指缝
哪样地，去尽情演奏证人不是人

那就是消息了

月亮集体地出现了，明天是从那边升起的
太晚了是指还有明天，但那是它们的明天
它们的迟到，就是今天的节日了。一阵
只准向前的痛楚，校正罗盘的指针，并
让时间的某一点，在现在成为准时，那
就是仅剩于枝上的几个主意之一——突然

3

One o'clock in the morning, the light has scattered to the outskirts,
     I stare at you, you
Also stare at me, in that patch of fog I left you, I listen closely to
Clouds, listen closely to the sky, and listen closely to the sound of flowing
     water as you clean the leaves

     "This civilization must go on standing dauntless"

A four-limbed woman strewn with sea horses floats into view, immediately
Dissolves like a tablet, passes by, to be retained by your body
It created my memory: You and I, were two
Stones, embracing on the lintel of a big opera house

     Now that is waiting

When dark night starts out from daytime, many parallel European rivers
Are like a bow stopped on a violin, waiting for a pair of hands
To come running, the same way that the gods only at night seek women's
     hand sowing
And thus, to passionately play and prove man is not man

     Now that's news

Moonlight collectively appears. Tomorrow will rise from there
Too late is fingers still having a tomorrow, but that is their tomorrow
Their late arrival, is today's holiday. A
Sore spot only allowed forward, rectifies the compass needle, and
Makes some moment or other in time, become the correct time of the
     present, now
That's only just one of the several ideas left over on the branch — suddenly

4

比一个男人高，又比一个男人的中指短
被留声机的曲柄摇着，世界的缺陷
造人的第一个声音——是一个病句
让看到的比听到的远，只远一点

　　　"但不许说静默只是静默"

这夜静得无人可以拾起沙子，老女人
死去的屋里，有一股秋天的皮革味
我听到尘埃离开她时的叹息，一阵冬天的
向下的低音音符，就停在琴弦的末端

　　　"把我像空气一祥地放走吧"

除了肉体的死亡，一切死亡都停止了
你的离去让树变成了谜语，而你曾是
哪条河流？当你数到颈上的第三颗钮扣时
我们的道路，仍是远离兄弟姐妹的同一只鞋

　　　"要走的只是节省而已了"

在土地更为突出路的时候，里程不再重要了
它曾对抗两个瞎子同时流出的泪
它们来自太阳密集的窟窿，和一本书
敞开时，继续洒向牧场的月光……

4

Taller than a man, and shorter than a man's middle finger
Cranked up by a gramophone handle, the world's shortcoming
Creating man's first sound — is a faulty sentence
Making what is seen farther than what is heard, only a little farther

"But one must not say silence is only silence"

This night is so silent no one may gather up sand, the old woman's
Dead room, has a whiff of autumn leather shoes about it
I hear the sigh of when dust takes its leave of her, a blast of
Descending bass notes, stops at the end of the string

"Let me go like air"

Apart from death of the flesh, all death has stopped
Your leaving made trees turn into riddles, and which river
Were you? When you counted to the third button on the collar
Our path, thereupon was distant from the shared shoe of the brothers
        and sisters

"What wants to go is thrift and no more"

When the earth boasts such prominent roads, the milestone is no
        longer important
It resisted two blindmen's simultaneously flowing tears
They come from the sun's concentrated holes, and when a book
Is opened right up, keep on shedding towards the moonlit pastureland…

1996

小麦的光芒

摘三十年前心爱的樱桃，挑故乡
运来的梨，追射向青春的那支箭
世上，还有另一种思念
没有马送我回来，用留在门上的
三下叩门声，人们为我命名：
　　　小麦的，小麦的

　　　　小麦的光芒

走过中国城的酱菜园，高丽蓼店，
棺材行，看我的前半生怎样
从一片麦地走出，羞愧的时刻
也是幸福的时刻，黄昏的分分秒秒
从红绸子店中闪耀的，依旧是

　　　　小麦的光芒

为插于背后的那把铲子伫立，耳中
一再回荡群山的轰鸣，一阵
老人间的亲嘴声，被输入时间
整座高原，仍是一阵低沉的鼓声
北方的声音，过往的光荣，怎样地
全靠一只铜锤，从万张脊背上擂响

　　　　小麦的光芒

RADIANCE OF WHEAT

Picking thirty-year-old treasured cherries, choosing the home country
Shipped-in pears, chasing arrow shot into youth
On earth, there is another memory
No horse brought me, with the sound of three
Knocks left on the door, people named me:
      Wheat, wheat

        The radiance of wheat

Walking past Chinatown's pickle factory, Korean ginseng shop,
Coffin makers, see how my life so far has been
Walking out from a wheat field, a moment of shame
Yet a moment of happiness also, the minutes and seconds of sundown
Shining out from the red silk shop, just like it used to shine

        The radiance of wheat

Stand still for a shovel stuck in the back, in the ear
A blast of valley-echoing thunder, a smack of
A kiss exchanged between old people, imported time
A whole plateau, remains a profound drumbeat
Northern sounds, passing glory, how come
All relies on a copper hammer, banging out on thousands of backbones

        The radiance of wheat

在颤抖的，只有肉颤抖的远方
一片左手写字的云，父亲的灵魂
移过国王的荒冢，挤进麦田上空的旋涡
让交错的电线怎样扯，也扯不开

小麦的光芒

站到老树林向夕阳驹躬的路口
五谷的影子从墙上掠过，手中的
活计，拿起又放下，该是
为年轻人擦泪的时候了?而
又一次忍着，而忍也忍不住，想也
不敢想，看也不用看，用一张
最名贵的桦树皮，换也不肯换

小麦的光芒

一阵日落时分落叶的冷战，即使
牙床上已长满墓碑，也还是
从死亡的深层背出了煤;即使
本来可以覆盖死人脚面上的
那点光，已经亮得像鞋油，像弟弟
头上的伤疤一样，电闪激化的
盐，也还能在皮肤上结晶

小麦的光芒

In the shivering distance, where only flesh shivers
A cloud writing left-handed, father's soul
Passes over the king's deserted grave, penetrates the whirlpool
      above the wheat field
Makes interweaved electric cables pull, but not succeed in pulling apart

      The radiance of wheat

Stand at the crossroads where the old tree shoots arrows at the setting sun
The shadows of five valleys brush across the wall, a handful of
Needlework, snatched up then cast down, surely
For when the youth wipe away their tears? And
Once more suffer, but suffer yet not stand to suffer, think yet
Not dare to think, look with no need to look, with a piece
Of the rarest of birch barks, exchange yet do not want to exchange

      The radiance of wheat

A tremor of a falling leaf at nightfall, even if
Gums are replete with tombstones, it is still
Coal carried up from deepest seam of death; even if
At first one could conceal on the dead man's foot
That spot of light, already shining like boot polish, just like brother's
Scar on his head, lightning sharpened
Salt, on the skin can still also crystallize

      The radiance of wheat

那就是你——腰里被蚊子叮过的一点
还在吸引我，从我身上渗出的每一滴汗
也还是一名小伙子，你站到我脚上
大地还会移动，马眨眼时
整个大草原，还能再翻一个过

小麦的光芒

总是有一块麦田还在动感情，像某个
女人的内分泌，还有秋天蚯蚓的味道
还在把因远离地脉而变得寒冷的东西
翻出来——就像你脸上的那颗痣
那早死的，已死的，死定的一年，还在
被流血的指甲抓着，抓住，抓紧
　　抓紧时辰啊

小麦的光芒

当农人赶着走向规范的马，麦田
也在显示空白，一如才能的离去啊
北方的脏话，突然停止
马粪中的稻草，飞向天空
马死前，马鬃已经朝天飞卷
而马蹄声中依然有语气，有语法
有预感:还有诗行啊

小麦的光芒

Now that's you — that spot on your waist bitten by a mosquito
Still fascinates me, every drop of sweat that seeps out of my body
Is still a youngster, you stand on my feet
Mother earth may still move, when the horse winks,
The whole vast plain, can again still flip over

The radiance of wheat

There is always a patch of wheat field still stirring the emotions, like some
Woman's hormones, and there is the taste of the autumn earthworm
Still churning up things turned cold because far from the veins of the earth
—— just like that mole on your face
That long dead, already dead, definitely dead year, still
Clutched at by bleeding fingernails, clutched hold of, clutched tight
        Ah, the moment of clutching tight

The radiance of wheat

When farmers spur on the horse moving towards the norm, the wheat field
Also manifest emptiness, ah, just like the departure of talent
Foul language of the north, suddenly stops
Rice stalks midst the horse dung, fly towards the sky
Before the horse dies, the horse's mane has already flown skywards
And still in the sound of the hooves is the tone of language, the syntax
        of language,
There is prescience: ah, and there is a line of poetry

The radiance of wheat

向着有烟囱矗立的麦田倾斜
也向冻裂的防护林致敬，星群
又一次升起，安抚拂动的羊毛
马奶在桶中摇晃着，批评
又一个早晨，在这样地展开：
是诗行，就得再次炸开水坝

小麦的光芒

闪电是个白色的织布人，毫不理会
午后一阵高过一阵的劈柴声
密林才是歌手，唱瓦沟里的草
先于我而知道的，竖琴被搂于割草人
怀中时唱过的，唱光所知道的
先于光所知道的，先于知道的
　　而知道了所有的

小麦的光芒

Leaning towards a wheat field on which a chimney stands erect
And saluting the forest that protects against the chapping cold, stars
Rise once again, placate the floating sheep's wool
Horse milk ripples in the pail, criticizes
Yet another morning, unfolds in this way:
It's a line of poetry, must once again blow open the dyke

   The radiance of wheat

Lightning is a white-colored weaver, who pays no heed
In the afternoon peals of ever louder thunder
The dense forest is now a singer, singing the grass in the gutters
Knew before me, sang the time when the harp was clasped in the grass cutter's
Embrace, sang what the light knows
Before what the light knew, before knowing
   Yet knew all

   The radiance of wheat

1996

既

以失望为夜莺，就得在象牙的回声里歌唱了
只是不能问，要唱多久才能变为蝴蝶

那就在船夫的腋窝里搔着，去指挥乐队吧
去摘取浮动于乐谱中的柠檬，帮助冰
打开鱼池，随马在废弃的浴盆内饮水
抬头，在经过处理的空旷中，把
病院深度的蓝，擦得更亮，奔跑于
一根根燃烧的火柴头的最尖端
随每一个瞬间，立即变为传统。

SINCE

Taking pessimism for a nightingale, it must sing within an ivory echo
Only it can't make a sound, it needs to sing many times before
        becoming a butterfly

Now it itches in the boatman's armpit, maybe goes conducting
        an orchestra
Goes to pick a lemon floating on the score, helps ice
Break open the fish pond, drinks with the horses from
        the discarded bathtub
Raises its head, passes through worked-over open space, polishes
Brighter the deep blue of the clinic, runs at
The most pointed burning match head
Follows each instant, immediately turns into tradition.

1998

这是被谁遗忘的天气

意味着不会再有什么被记起
也不会再有什么值得一再消逝

画在船头的眼睛望着前方
路上，仅有马匹归来

正是此时，滚动的云朵
突然跟上大管风琴的呼啸

每一个瞬间的溃败，涌进它
钥匙已不必猜测，雷霆从不空虚

大海不光数沙子，有人
还在写信，只是不再寄出——

THIS IS WHOSE FORGOTTEN WEATHER

Meaning cannot again have anything to be remembered
Nor have anything again worthy of repeated disappearance

The eyes painted on the bow of the ship stare ahead
On the road, there are only horses returning

Just at this moment, rolling clouds
Suddenly catch up with the whistle of the large pipe organ

Each flashing defeat, rushes into it
The key no longer needs to be guessed, the thunder is never hollow

The ocean does not only count sand, there are people
Still writing letters, it's just that they're no longer sent ——

1998

无题

天空招唤不已，文明
与其不配，起点震撼终点
星辰运算，时间失效

攥紧药，恒星不必巨大
刺向内，衣钩向下，不只
向着西方，所以向着世界

全碎了，不再纪录，流血
止血，光不显，也不停
如数流进资源，再透出人声

租期到了，听力丧尽，一份
总谱，星罗棋布，除了
启示，全在断语之间……

TITLELESS POEM

The summons of the sky has not stopped, civilization,
Does not accompany it, the starting point shakes the destination
The stars calculate, time ceases to count

Clenching tight the medicine, perseverance has no need to be enormous
Stabbing inwards, clothes hooks downwards, not just
Westwards, thus towards the world

All is fragmented, never again to be noted, bleeding
Stop bleeding, the light is not apparent, but is not out
All the resources flowing in, once more exit through voices

The lease is up, hearing is deafened, a page of
Musical score, scattered, excepting
Inspiration, all is between conclusions…

1999

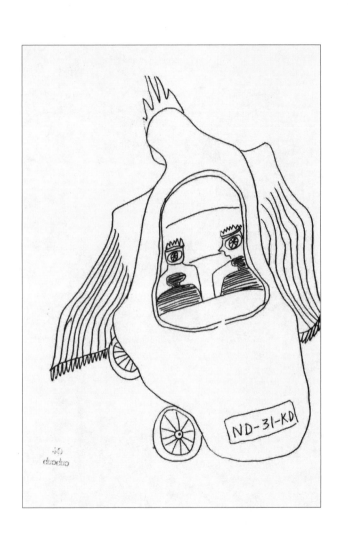

duoduo